THE PAST

ARCHAEOLOGY IN YOUR OWN BACKYARD

BY BRUCE PORELL

Line drawings by Bruce Elliott

 ADDISON-WESLEY

18, J57 X

Library of Congress Cataloging in Publication Data

Porell, Bruce, 1947 –
  Digging the past.

  Includes index.
  SUMMARY: Stories, suggested activities, and games
introduce the many facets of and the people involved in
archaeology.
  1. Archaeology – Juvenile literature. [1. Archae-
ology] I. Elliott, Bruce, 1938-   II. Title.
CC171.P67   930'.1   79-18741
ISBN 0-201-05859-6
ISBN 0-201-05860-X pbk.

The photographs in this book are reproduced courtesy of the following:
Cover, pages 62–63, 67, 86, 96–97, 99, 116   Tell el-Hesi Expedition, photos by
Theodore A. Rosen.   Pages viii–1   Joseph Weiler   Pages 5, 33, 42–43, 59,
61, 81, 107, 111, 112, 113, 115, 136, 139, 152   Bruce Porell.   Pages 6–7
Peabody Museum, Harvard University, photograph by unknown.   Pages 8–9
Robert Arnold.   Pages 17, 73, 75, 76–77   Old Sturbridge Village Research
Library, Original Manuscript Collection, photos by Robert Arnold.   Pages 18,
85   The Metropolitan Museum of Art, photographs by Harry Burton.   Pages 38–39
The Metropolitan Museum of Art, Photography Egyptian Expeditions.
Pages 20–21, 25, 27, 50–51, 124   The Bettman Archive   Pages 28–29, 30 Ford
Motor Company   Page 52   Drawing by J. W. Whymper in Heinrich Schliemann,
Trojan Antiquities (London, John Murray, 1874)   Pages 57, 68, 102–103
Old Sturbridge Village Archaeology, John Worrell   Pages 71, 90, 104, 129,
130–131   Old Sturbridge Village Archaeology, Bruce Elliott   Page 119
New York Public Library   Page 110-111 A Shorter Version of the Vertabrate
Body by Romer (W. B. Saunders Company, Philadelphia, PA)

FOR
LINDA,
WITH LOVE.

CONTENTS

SECTION IV
SOLVING THE MYSTERY 97

Acknowledgments

My love and appreciation to Linda Yorton, my wife, for her help and support through the writing of this book. Dr. John Morrell and Dr. Linda Ammons both took time from busy lives to help and support a friend. For this, and for their excellent advice and technical assistance, my sincerest appreciation. Bruce Elliott gave of his time, patience and talent to help me with his skillful and creative line drawings. Thank you, Bruce.

Thanks, also, to four of my students who helped me illustrate parts of this book; Heather Taylor, Linea Rowe, Jim Crawford, and Shannon Bertrand, my appreciation. And to Bob Arnold, a good friend, who gave of his time and photographic talents on some spur-of-the-moment ventures. Thank you, Bob.

My warmest appreciation to Elizabeth Orton Jones who convinced me that writing can be fun. To Mary K. Harmon and all the other nice people at Addison-Wesley, thank you for your help in putting this book together.

PREFACE

This is a book about archaeology. It is more than an explanation of what archaeology is, more than a picture book of all the wonderful objects that have been found buried in dirt around the world, and more than a survey of the famous archaeologists and their contributions to the field.

Here you will find out why anyone would want to dig up a bunch of broken pots or would study the collapsed walls of an old city. You will discover how these objects are found and dug up, and how the archaeologist constructs a people's way of life from these clues. You will find things to do and think about that will help sharpen your own skills.

Digging the Past is a book that will start you thinking like a detective, reading evidence from the past, and using your imagination just as the archaeologists do.

Archaeology is the Science of Finding, collecting, and studying the Material remains of our past.

SECTION I

DIGGING THE
PAST

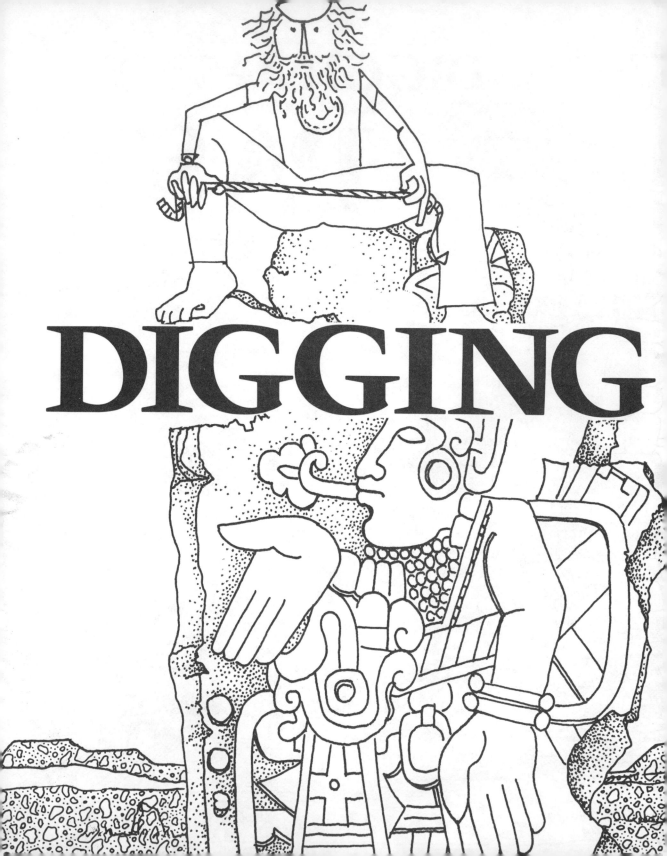

DIGGING

1. Clues for the Archaeologist

Archaeologists study the material remains of our past. Material remains, called artifacts, are simply the objects used by people in their everyday lives. Artifacts are the pots we cook in and the dishes we eat from. Artifacts are the chairs and tables in your living room, the rubber ball in your bedroom, the toothbrush in the rack over your bathroom sink, and the chicken bones you threw away after supper last night. Artifacts are everywhere. They are our tools, toys, furniture, decorations, gadgets, and weapons. Even the buildings we live and work in are artifacts. Look around you. You are wearing artifacts and you are surrounded by them.

Is the tree outside your window an artifact? No, not unless you cut it down and hollow it out to make yourself a canoe; remove a branch and whittle a whistle; boil the roots for tea; or burn the wood for heat. Wood is an obvious source of artifacts. Hundreds of artifacts have been made from trees.

3

2. Wastebasket Archaeology

Artifacts provide information about the people who use them. For instance, you can learn about people from "reading" their wastebasket.

Try this. Spread some newspaper on a flat place and dump your kitchen wastebasket out. The kitchen wastebasket is usually the one with the most interesting and diverse artifacts. You can find everything from bills to banana peels, newspapers to tomato soup cans.

THE ARTIFACTS

Pretend you know nothing about the people who use your kitchen except what you can learn from the evidence you find in their wastebasket. Try to answer some of these questions as you sort through your pile. Remember, you can answer a question only if you have the evidence to support your answer.

Look through food scraps, and read labels on cans, bottles, and other packaging. What kind of diet do these people have? Are the foods homegrown or imported? If they are imported, from where?

Is there any evidence about the kind of fuel used to heat or do other jobs in the house? Are there any oil bills or electric bills?

Are there any newspapers or pamphlets that show the type of community these people live in?

What kinds of games do these people play? Is there a sports page or broken plastic ball? Can you figure out any rules of the game you have found from the artifact you are examining?

Do these people use money? Can you figure out how their money works?

Maybe wastebaskets aren't your area of interest. Perhaps you are more an attic person or a car-trunk person. These and lots of other places are fun to explore from the archaeologist's point of view. Play Sherlock Holmes in each place you examine. Treat each artifact as a clue that can yield a piece of the puzzle you are trying to complete.

What can a raisin box tell you about the kind of society you live in?

3. Pieces of the Puzzle

We have historians to write history books. Why do we need archaeologists, too? What information can the archaeologist contribute that the historian cannot?

Historians rely on information gathered from written sources. Historians collect the information from old documents and piece together a picture of a particular group of people living in a particular period in history. This picture is the historians' opinion, based on the best facts they can find.

Written sources are important, but writing goes back only about 5000 years and many old documents have been lost or destroyed. Just a couple of hundred years ago most people were illiterate. Those that could write wrote about gods, wars, and kings. People's everyday experiences were not considered important enough to write about. Even after writing became common, people still didn't write much about what was happening to them. So there are a lot of holes in our historical jigsaw puzzle.

6

Archaeologists rely on information gathered from the ground. They use their special knowledge of how to read the *strata* — or layers of earth — and the artifacts collected there. Experts from many fields of science help archeologists understand the clues that the ground has to offer. Then from the bits and pieces they have been able to put together, archaeologists, too, form a picture.

By combining the information gathered by the historian and the archaeologist, we get a better picture of the past. The jigsaw puzzle is clearer, more probable, and more complete.

A view in the Island of Ulieta with a double canoe and a boat-home.

4. Potsherds Talk

Artifacts are more than just the "things" people make for their use. Artifacts represent the ideas of a culture. (Culture, as archaeologists use the word, means any group of people who share a common way of life.) Each culture has its own idea of how something — a spear, a pot, or a basket — should look. For instance, spears made by the Great Lakes Indians are different from those made by Indians from northwest Canada. Each group had its own idea of how a spear should look and passed this design down from generation to generation.

A culture's idea of how something should look was based not only on the material available but also on the shape of the object and on the decoration added to it. A common kind of decoration was a religious symbol, such as the cross found on many artifacts in Christian cultures.

Decorations do not have to be painted on. Church bells are a form of decoration for a church. Before the widespread use of the clock, the church bell told people when to come to church services. Today many churches still have bells, and bell ringing is a symbolic reminder of the church's call to prayer.

In modern industrialized society it is very difficult to identify artifacts as belonging to one specific culture. Mass production and heavy trade between countries have standardized and blended the cultural identities of artifacts.

Many early Hopi Indian potters used birds and parts of birds, such as wings and feathers, as decorations on their pottery.

9

5. Preservation and Decay

When archaeology is discussed, people unfortunately think only of long ago and far away. True, many of the original archaeological studies concentrated on sites in such places as Africa, Mesopotamia, Egypt, and the Greek and Roman Empires. Everyone marvels at the spectacular treasures found in those excavations because some objects lasted almost intact for thousands of years. Today many archaeologists are just as interested in digging closer to home at sites that date back only a hundred years.

Even a hundred years is long enough for much evidence to be destroyed. Artifacts that the archaeologist is working with have often been subjected to nature's forces. Some materials stand up to corrosion and decay better than others.

Cloth, paper, and wood are easily destroyed by dampness, fire, and insects. These materials decay and return to the soil. They can become difficult or impossible to recognize after only a few years.

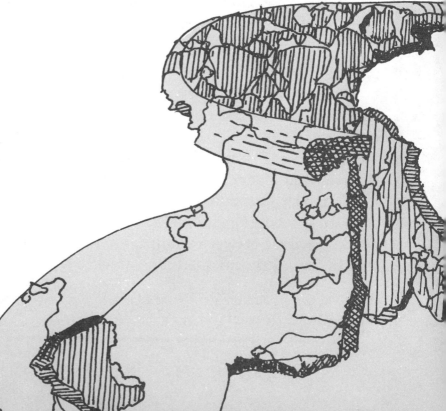

Common metals, such as iron, copper, and bronze, will rust and corrode, depending upon the amount of moisture they come in contact with. If kept reasonably dry, they may survive intact and need only chemical treatment to restore them to good condition.

Pottery and stone are the materials that survive the longest. On archaeological sites pots and stone tools are often the most commonly found artifacts.

The environment can preserve or destroy artifacts. Extreme dryness or freezing conditions preserve artifacts for long periods of time. On the other hand, high humidity, acid soil conditions (like those in pine forests or agricultural lands), and bacteria in the soil contribute to quick decay.

Modern plastics and synthetics may rival pottery and stone in resisting corrosion and decay. Some of these new materials will be around for ten thousand years before breaking down and returning to the soil.

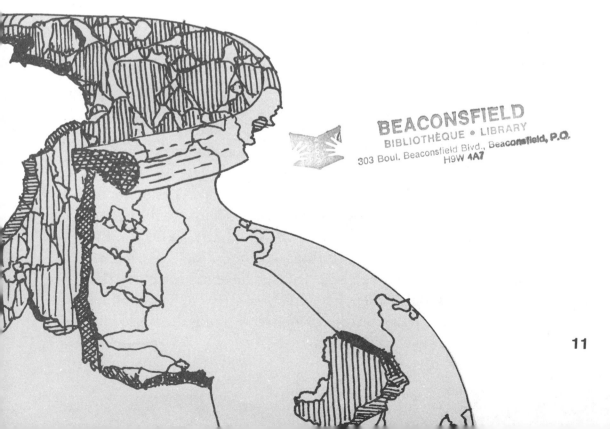

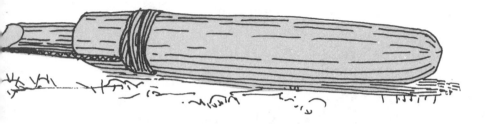

6. Who Were the Haida?

This picture shows five artifacts belonging to people from a single culture. The sea canoe, used by the Haida Indians, could carry up to fourteen people. The Haida lived along the coast of North America where Washington and Oregon are now. Fish were an important source of food for these Indians. On a dig, what clues might the archaeologist-detective expect to find? Racks for drying fish? Clam shells? Can you think of any artifacts that the Indians might have made from fish and shellfish remains?

Some of the Haida tools are pictured. You can see how the wooden handles were attached to the stone and bone pieces. There is a stone *maul* or hammer with a handle, an adz that works like a plane to smooth wood, and a chisel. The stone object in the foreground is ten inches high and made of stone. The object might be a chess piece or a salt shaker. What do you think the object was used for? With their woodworking tools, what besides canoes might the Haida Indians have made to help them survive? What tools, weapons, and other artifacts would make survival easier for a primitive group living along the rugged coastline of the northwestern United States?

The stone artifact pictured in the illustration is a hand maul used for crushing and pounding.

13

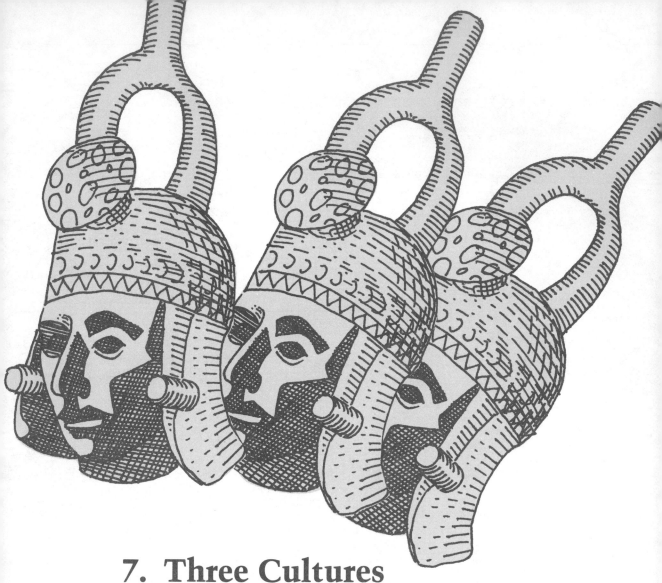

7. Three Cultures

Pictured here are seven artifacts that represent three groups of people. To separate the artifacts, look for similarities in the materials used to make them. Then look for any styles or patterns that seem to be used in more than one artifact.

Now decide which objects belong together because they were made by people of the same culture. What are these artifacts? Who do you think might have made them? How are the three cultures different from each other?

The sword, helmet, and pike-axe are Spanish.
The stirrup-mouthed jar, temple front, and stone stool are Mayan.
The totem pole belongs to a northwestern American Indian tribe.

15

8. The Apprentice

The skills and crafts that were important to early cultures were passed from father to son and from mother to daughter within the family. At times, however, young people were apprenticed to a craftsperson to learn a special trade. The expert craftsperson might teach how to make a hammer or a horseshoe. The young apprentice spent years learning to make the object exactly as the expert did.

These apprenticeships meant long hours of work for the boy or girl with no pay other than room and board and the privilege of learning a trade. Here is an excerpt from an apprenticeship contract for three-year-old Isaac Mahurin to learn farming.

This Indenture Witnesseth

That Thomas Willis, Thomas Whitman, Jacob Haywood, Amos Keith and Shepard Fisk, Selectmen of the Town of Bridgwater in the County of Plymouth in New England, by, and with the Consent of Two of his Majesties Justices of the Peace for the County aforesaid do put and bind Isaac Mahurin son of Benjamin Mahurin late of Bridgwater aforesaid dec'd: to be an Apprentice unto Sarah Allen of Bridgwater aforesaid Widow to learn the Art, Trade or Mystery of Husbandry, and with her the said Sarah Allen and her Heirs after the Manner of an Apprentice, to Dwell and Serve, from the Day of the Date hereof, for and during the full and just Term of Seventeen Years and twenty eight Days next ensuing or until he shall arrive to the age of Twenty one Years, and fully to be compleat and ended. . .

Read the remainder of this indenture document from the original shown on the next page.

16

This Indenture Witnesseth,

That *Thomas Willis Thomas Whitman Jacob Hayward Amos Keith and Shepard Fisk Selectmen of the Town of Bridgwater in the County of Plymouth in New England, By*

~~—~~, and with the Consent of *Two of his Majesties Justices of the Peace for the County aforesaid*

Isaac Mahurin son of Benjamin Mahurin late of Bridgwater aforesd. decd.

doth put and bind ʌ to be an Apprentice unto *Sarah Allen of Bridgwater aforesd. Widow* —

of Husbandry

To learn the Art, Trade or Mystery, and with *her* the said *Sarah Allen & her Heirs* — after the Manner of an Apprentice; to Dwell and Serve, from the Day of the Date hereof, for and during the full and just Term of *Seventeen Years & twenty eight Days next ensuing or until he shall arrive to the Age of twenty one years* ~~next ensuing~~, and fully to be compleat and ended. During all which said Term, the said Apprentice *his* said *Mistress* honestly and faithfully shall Serve, *her* Secrets keep close, *her* lawful and reasonable Commands every where gladly Do and Perform; Damage to *his* — said *Mistress he* — shall not wilfully do, *his said Mistress's* Goods *he* shall not waste, embezel, purloine or lend unto others, nor suffer the same to be wasted or purloined, but to *his* Power shall forthwith discover and make known the same unto *his* said *Mistress* — Taverns or Ale-houses *he* shall not frequent; at Cards, Dice, or any other unlawful Game *he* shall not play; Fornication *he* shall not commit, nor Matrimony contract with any Person during the said Term. From *his sd Mistress's* — Service *he* shall not at any Time unlawfully absent *himself* — but in all Things as a good, honest and faithful Servant and Apprentice, shall bear and behave *himself* — towards *his* said *Mistress & all hers* — during the full Term *aforesd:*

commencing as aforesaid.

And the said *Sarah Allen* — for *her self & Heirs* — Doth Covenant, & Promise, ~~————~~ in Manner and Form following, THAT IS TO SAY, That *she* will teach *hers* Apprentice, or cause *him* to be Taught by the best Ways and Means that *she or they* may or can, the Trade, Art or Mystery of *Husbandry & also to Read & write* — (if *her* said Apprentice be capable to learn) and will find and provide for and unto *her* said Apprentice, good and sufficient *Meat, Drink, Apparel, Washing & Lodging, & all other necessaries both in Sickness & in Health* — fitting for an Apprentice during the said Term; and at the End of said Term to dismiss said Apprentice *with two suits of Apparel for all Parts of the Body, One fit for Lords-Days, the other for working-Days, suitable for such an Apprentice*

In Testimony whereof, The said Parties to these present Indentures have interchangeably set their Hands and Seals, the *First* — Day of *January* in the *Third* — Year of the Reign of Our Sovereign Lord *George the Third* by the Grace of GOD, King of Great-Britain, France and Ireland, and in the Year of our Lord, One Thousand Seven Hundred and *Sixty Three.*

Sarah Allen

Signed, Sealed and Delivered
in Presence of *and allowed*
by us of two of his Majesties
Justices of the peace for the
County aforesaid
Daniel Johnson
John Willis

9. How and Why Artifacts Were Buried

Why after so many years do we find artifacts lying on the floors of village buildings and in the rubble of streets? How did these artifacts get buried in the first place?

Most of the time, broken or worn out tools and other artifacts were thrown out the door or dumped in a backyard trash pit. New objects were made or traded for while the old ones were buried by sand or leaves, or covered by vegetation growing over and around them, or broken down by wind and rain.

Even in the most ancient times people buried their dead. The archaeologist often finds charms, ornaments, tools, or weapons buried with their owners. Some powerful rulers even went so far as to have servants buried with them. These cultures believed that tools, weapons, or even servants would be useful to the dead in their afterlife.

The burial rites of different cultures are fascinating. Your library has books that tell of cultures that buried only the skulls of their dead, or buried just the men, or buried both men and women but at different depths. What are some of the things that were buried with Egyptian Pharaohs? What can you find out about the burial practices of American Indian tribes? Look up the term "necropolis" and see if you can find any examples.

Sometimes people buried objects such as money and collections of tools. Burying something was one of the best ways to safeguard possessions against thieves.

Rarely the archaeologist will dig a site and find almost everything intact and in place. The artifacts are undisturbed because the people suffered some great catastrophe, such as a sudden invasion, a terrible epidemic, or a drought that destroyed the residents. Although terrible for the people, these events provide an archaeologist the greatest kind of find. But even such finds often leave only partial information after may years because nature and later human activities can cause many things to be lost.

10. The Black Death

In the mid-fourteenth century, a group of Genoese merchants, returning from China with precious silks and furs, were reportedly attacked by a band of Tartars. The merchants took shelter in a small, walled town, which the Tartars promptly surrounded. For three years neither side was able to make any headway against the other until the Tartars hit upon a diabolical plan. Instead of catapulting rocks over the walls of the town, the Tartars began hurling in the corpses of their own men who had died of bubonic plague.

The whole town became infected. The Tartars disappeared, probably because of their own losses from the disease, and the merchants at once ran to their ships. The survivors of this voyage, who landed in such cities as Genoa and Venice, infected everyone they came in contact with.

People fled to every corner of Europe to escape the plague, and so spread it everywhere they went. In five years, two-thirds of the population of Europe was infected. Over half of the sick, about 25 million people, died.

Those who tried to escape by sea discovered that the disease followed them. Only much later was it discovered that the European black rat carried the plague bacteria. This rat lives in close contact with people and the bite of its flea was the infecting agent.

Bubonic plague was a major catastrophe, but disease is sometimes the reason that archaeological sites are left intact.

The bite of a small flea, carrying the Bubonic plague bacillus, was responsible for the deaths of millions of people.

11. Bog Burials

In a bog called Tolund Mose, high in the hills of Denmark, a man's body was discovered during peat cutting. He was found seven feet down. His only remaining clothing was a leather belt and a skull cap. Part of a braided leather rope encircled his neck. The man had been hanged.

The body was wonderfully preserved, tanned like a leather hide by the chemicals in the peat. When the stomach was opened, the remnants of a mixture of grain and wild seeds showed what he had eaten before death. A growth of stubble on his chin showed that he had not shaved for three or four days before he died.

Other bodies were found in bogs in the same area around Jutland, Denmark. Among the bodies were a man with his throat cut, a young girl who had been blindfolded, and a man that had been strangled with a hazel wand. All were naked or scantily clothed, and each had met with a violent death. Their date is somewhere between 300 BC and 300 AD. They were probably executed as criminals or as religious sacrifices. There is some support for the sacrifice theory because Celtic religious practices included placing offerings in bogs or in water.

12. A City Preserved

The city of Pompeii, Italy, is an example of an area that was struck by a great natural catastrophe.

Mount Vesuvius had erupted in AD 63 and damaged Pompeii, Naples, and Herculaneum; but the people, believing that an eruption couldn't happen again, rebuilt and stayed on. Then in AD 79 disaster struck. The eruption came so suddenly and so violently that many of the people did not have time to escape. The air filled with hot ashes, cinders, stones, and poisonous fumes. Some people were trapped in their homes as the volcanic ash buried the entire city. Others, trying to escape, were killed by the poisonous fumes and covered by the hot, wet ashes. As these ashes cooled and hardened, they made molds of the bodies inside. By pouring plaster into these molds, archaeologists have been able to make perfect casts of the individuals who were killed. Many casts are so detailed that the expression of agony shows on the face of the victim. The next page shows a petrified body from Pompeii.

The eruption destroyed the cities of Stabiae and Herculaneum, too. The mud and lava that covered these areas changed the course of the Sarno River and raised the beach so that the sites of these cities disappeared until later rediscovery. Pompeii was buried for almost 1700 years.

About one hundred years ago the Italian government began a systematic uncovering of the whole city of Pompeii. It was decided later not to remove the treasures being found there, but to keep them at the site and to restore the buildings. Today visitors can walk around sections of the oval, walled city and marvel at the streets paved with lava blocks that still have the ancient wheel ruts from carts that did business in the city. You can view the open square in the center of the city, the two theaters, a gladiator's court, and several, large public baths. Thousands of objects are on display there and at the National Museum at Naples, about thirteen miles from Pompeii.

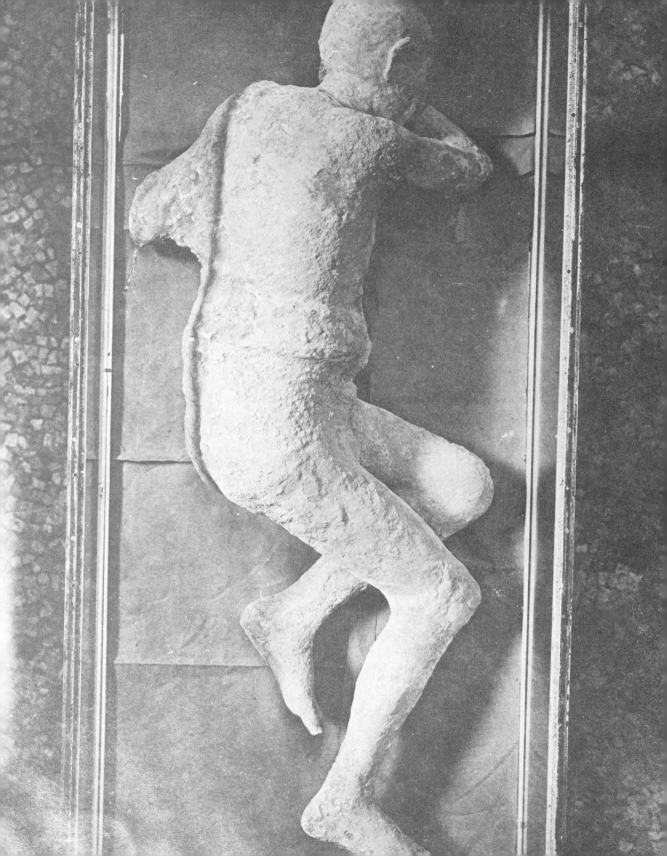

13. Dead Sea Scrolls

Beginning in 1947, archaeologists discovered eleven caves in the foothills near the northwestern shores of the Dead Sea in Palestine. Some of the caves were natural and some were dug. In several of the caves were found ancient scrolls, many of them books of the Old Testament. This was an amazing archaeological find because these scrolls are at least 1000 years older than any other Old Testament manuscripts found previously.

Cave I held the great scroll of Isaiah; this scroll was seven and a half yards long, and was the only complete manuscript found. Of the seven other scrolls found in Cave I, some were quite large but incomplete. There were also about 40 other manuscripts, but they were in hundreds of tiny pieces. Cave IV held even more manuscripts, but these were found in over a hundred thousand fragments of varying sizes and states of preservation.

The reason for the better condition of the manuscripts in Cave I is that they had been placed in pottery jars while the manuscripts in Cave IV had simply been laid on the ground. The Cave IV scrolls had been attacked by soil bacteria, rats, white ants, and weevils.

Archaeologists were able to date the scrolls when a jar, identical to the ones in Cave I, was found in the floor of a room in an ancient ruin near the cave sites. On the floor beside the pot was a coin dating from AD 10. The scrolls had been hidden when the settlement was about to be invaded by the Romans. Archaeologists have dated the writing of the scrolls as no later than AD 68.

Restoring the Dead Sea Scrolls required patience and a delicate touch.

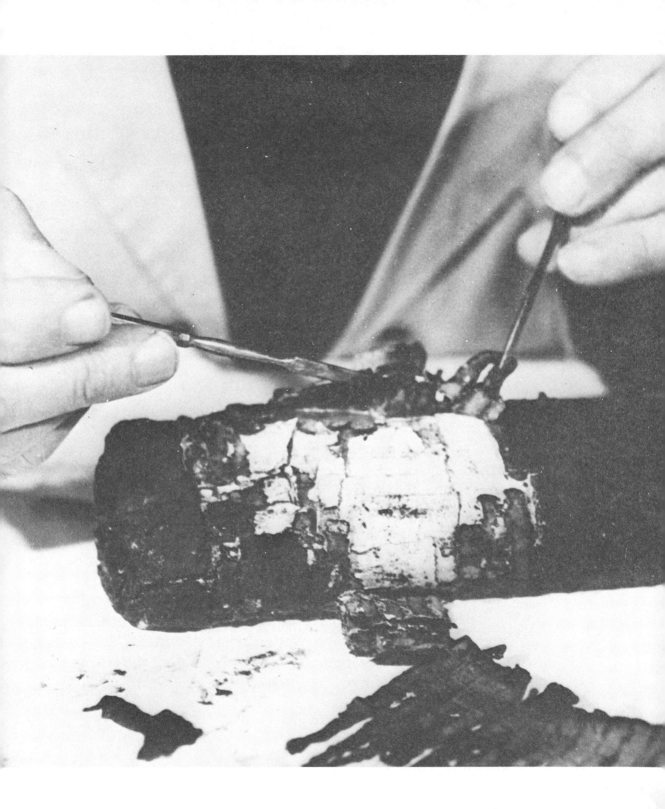

14. Dating

One of the most important facts the archaeologist must establish about the artifacts and fossils is how old they are. In order to draw proper conclusions about information uncovered at the dig, it is important to know what period the artifacts are from.

The methods used to date artifacts fall into two main categories: relative dating and absolute dating.

Methods of Relative Dating

Dating the strata An object found at a level known to be 2000 years old can reasonably be assumed to be 2000 years old or older. If an archaeologist were to dig up your house a hundred years from now, the artifacts found would all be at least a hundred years old. There would no doubt be some artifacts that were older because most of our possessions are not new. In fact, some of the objects in your house may be heirlooms passed down through generations.

Dating by typology Typology is the study of how artifacts changed from time to time. People who study types of artifacts are interested in how they were made, how they changed, and why they changed. The typologist learns to recognize the changes in artifacts just as you may learn to recognize changes in automobile styles from year to year.

Methods of Absolute Dating

Radio-carbon dating Radio-carbon dating is probably the

Can you guess which car is the oldest and which is the newest (cars A –I).
Check your guess on page 31.

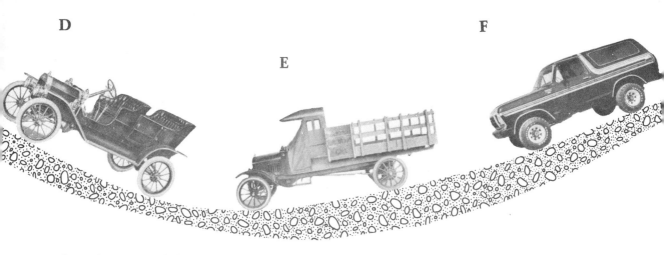

D

E

F

best-known of the dating methods. Scientists have learned to measure the balance between carbon 12 and carbon 14. Both of these carbons are found in a fixed ratio in *living* animals and plants. When a plant or animal dies, carbon 14 begins to change slowly into carbon 12 at a rate that can be measured. Half of the carbon 14 changes to carbon 12 in 5570 years. Half of the half left will take another 5570 years to change, and so on.

This method is fairly accurate for as far back as 50,000 years. Radio-carbon dating is not helpful when something must be dated to within 100 to 150 years. That is its limit of accuracy. For more recent times, other methods of absolute dating may better pin-point the date.

Other methods of absolute dating that are used in special cases are

Thermoluminescence, giving off light when heated, which is used to date pottery;
Potassium-argon, used for dating volcanic materials;
Obsidian hydration, used for dating chipped stone artifacts made from obsidian.

G   H   I

Dendrochronology, tree-ring dating. Growth in a tree is accomplished by a ring of cells, known as the cambium, just inside the bark. Each year (in temperate regions) new wood is added to the tree trunk by the multiplication of the cambium layer. In the summer, the cells produced by this layer are large and light in color. In winter, they get very small and grow close together; the result is a darker color. The contrasting light and dark layers produce what are called growth rings.

By counting these rings, we can determine the age of a tree as well as the relative amounts of sunlight and rainfall it received each year. Summers with lots of sunshine and rainfall would produce the greatest growth of new cells and therefore the largest space between the dark, winter rings.

Dendrochronologists have made charts of these growth rings for many different kinds of trees of all ages. When the archaeologist sends a sample of wood from the beams of an old building, the growth rings are compared with the charts. If the sample is a good one, the dating expert matches the beam's rings with rings on the charts and is able to date the piece of wood.

The difficulties in dating by tree rings are many. The dendrochronologist must have ring charts of the species of tree from which the sample comes. The charts must be made from trees having the same geographical location as that of the sample. A tree from Maine may have had different amounts of sunlight and rainfall in a particular year than a tree from Toronto, Canada. If the beam is from a Maine pine tree, the dater must have charts of Maine pine trees.

Unless the outer bark is on the sample, the specialist cannot accurately date the year the tree was cut down because the years are counted backward from the bark to the center of the tree. As more accurate charts are made, tree-ring dating will become an ever more useful tool.

Dendrochronology is easier to do than to spell. Find a tree that has been cut down and count the rings to find out how old it is. In which years did the sun shine and rain fall best for this tree? What kind of tree is it? You can make a tracing of these rings and the rings of other trees. This can be a beginning toward making your own tree-ring dating charts.

15. Personal Time Capsules

Today we sometimes purposely bury artifacts in *time capsules* to celebrate special events, such as the anniversaries of towns, cities, and countries. Time capsules are usually filled with artifacts that are both current and typical of the culture.

You can make a time capsule to bury that will be typical of you and your family. Carefully choose those artifacts that you feel tell your story best, and place them in a *waterproof* container. (Glass or plastic work well.) Years from now if you dig up your time capsule, you will find a record of your past life. You will be able to compare this record with your life in this future time and see changes in your lifestyle.

You may want to leave your time capsule as a possible find for some future archaeologist. If so, you'll want to include the kinds of information archaeologists are searching for. Here are a couple of ideas for artifacts that would give future archaeologists some good clues about the life you are living now.

Keep a diary for at least a week. Write down what happens to you each day during this week. Include subjects that you and your friends talk about during the week, information that you are studying in school each day, your after-school activities, television programs that you watch, what you eat for each meal, and anything else you can think of that describes your life during this week. Remember to write on at least one weekend.

If you have a camera or can borrow one, take pictures of people and artifacts that you are in contact with each day. These photographs will help fill in information about artifacts, like your typewriter or your mathbook, that you cannot put into your time capsule.

Include a test you took in school, a book that you enjoyed reading, a cassette tape of your voice and the voices of other members of your family, and your shoe size, jacket size, and pants size.

Keeping a special diary for placement in a personal time capsule.

What else can you think of that tells about you as you are now?

Put all your artifacts into the container, find a good spot, and bury your time capsule. Make a map of the exact location, and place the map in a book or other safe place. Don't hide the map so well that you will never find it.

When will you dig up your time capsule? In five years? Ten years? Or will you leave it for a future archaeologist to find?

16. Preserved in Mud?

In just a few minutes, this house and all its contents are going to be buried in a sudden, enormous mudslide. Pretend for the moment that the danger to this family is not known and they are not rescued.

If this site were to be dug up five hundred years from now, what would probably still be intact? Which artifacts do you think would survive the mold and mildew, insects and corrosion?

The people are artifacts too. They are artifacts of this household and of their culture. Let your imagination go. What objects might be in the people's pockets or ornamenting their bodies? Perhaps one person is wearing contact lenses. What objects might the archaeologist find that are not shown directly in this picture?

35

17. Drying Flowers

Plant tissue, as well as animal tissue, can be dried in sand. This method of drying flowers preserves their color for years.

Get some fine sand (beach sand is best) and clean it thoroughly by sifting and washing. Let it dry completely.

Into a box or large coffee can, place three inches of sand. Cut your flower with a three-inch stem and plant it immediately in the sand by poking a hole with a stick and placing the flower stem in the hole.

Then fill a cup with sand and carefully pour it around the flower, not on top of it, until the sand is level with the top petals. Spoon sand carefully over the petals; bury them an inch and a half under the sand.

After two weeks, carefully brush aside the sand and gently feel one of the petals. It should feel like straw. Remove the flower and gently tap the stem to remove sand sticking to the flower.
Use a soft paintbrush to remove any remaining sand.

18. Mummification

Early Egyptians believed that the continuation of a dead person's identity depended upon the preservation of the body. To this end, many Egyptians were mummified.

The process included the removal of the brain. With a long metal instrument, the brain was removed from the skull through the nostril, normally the left one. Then the heart, lungs, stomach, and liver were removed and placed in separate jars.

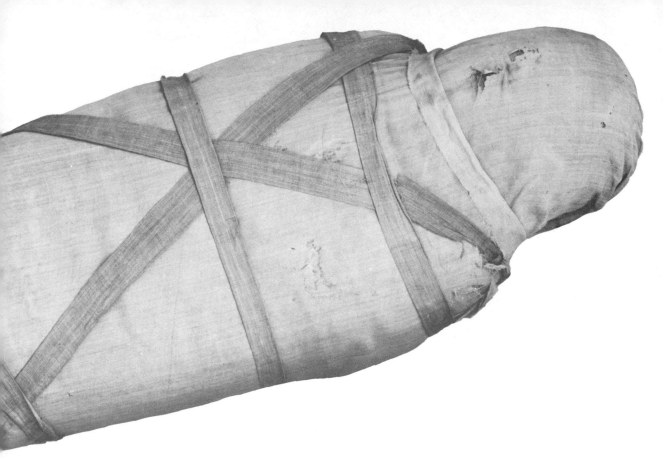

Mummy of Kharu-shery, Eygpt.

Next as much water as possible was removed from the body by placing it on a mat on the ground and packing it with crystals of natron. These acted as a purifier and a drying agent. When completely dried, the body was coated with resin and wrapped tightly in linen bandages. The entire process took about seventy days.

In extremely dry climates it is not too unusual to find that bodies buried in shallow graves have been preserved by *desiccation*, drying out. In parts of South America, bodies that have been preserved in this way are known as mummies.

39

19. Artifact Games

Here is a game to play with a friend or a group of kids who know each other and each other's family pretty well. Have every kid in the group bring a box of eight or ten artifacts that identify a member of his or her family. Pass the boxes around. Each person can write a guess for each box. Now let each box owner tell about his or her box. Were some of the boxes harder to guess than others?

40

Another artifact game goes like this: Let each member of your group bring in only one artifact from home. Then get together and make up an imaginary person who might use all of these artifacts. Take notes and write as complete a description as possible using only the information you can discover from the artifacts. Use cautious words like probably, possibly, sometimes, might, could, and so on, to describe your mystery person. If one of your artifacts is a coffee cup, you might write: "This person probably drank coffee or tea." You should not write: "This person definitely drank coffee or tea." You don't know that for sure. It's just possible that the coffee cup was used for hot chocolate and nothing else. How do you think you could find out what the cup was used for? (If a coffee can were among the artifacts it might lend strength to the coffee theory. But still the proof would not be definite.)

Archaeologists often don't know for sure what an artifact was used for because different cultures do things very differently. For example, what would an African Pygmy imagine a flip-top from a soda can to be?

Here's an exercise for your imagination and creativity. See how many uses you can think of for a junked car. You can use the car as a whole or take it apart piece by piece. Make a tire swing with the tires. (Tires have lots of uses. What else could you do with them?) Cut off the roof and plant a garden in the body of the car. Make a sculpture for your bedroom by glueing together parts from the engine.

How creative are you? Can you think of twenty-five uses? Fifty? One hundred?

SECTION II

THE SEARCH

1. Accidental Discovery

Hundreds of sites have been dug in places all over the world.

How did archaeologists know where to dig?

Occasionally a place to dig is located by accident: a farmer turns up artifacts while plowing a field, a worker discovers the ruins of a Roman temple under the streets of London, or a scholar traveling in the Egyptian desert sees the head of a sphinx protruding from the sand. There have been many such "lucky" finds in the history of archaeology.

In 1928 an Arab farmer struck the remains of a tomb while plowing his field near a large mound called Ras Shamra in Syria. He reported what he had found, and the following year a French archaeological group found that the farmer had discovered the site of an ancient town known as Ugarit.

Digging into the mound, the archaeologists learned that the site had been occupied five different times from the Neolithic period to the Late Bronze age. They found huge fortifications, temples, and an entire palace complete with cuneiform documents in three, ancient, known languages. The archaeologists also found documents written in an unknown language, very similar to ancient Hebrew and Phoenician languages. The unknown language was written in an alphabetic cuneiform script with 29 characters. Among the writings were epic poems recounting stories of the god Baal.

2. Clues to Location

Archaeologists don't leave the discovery of ancient sites to chance, especially today, when many sites are in danger of being forever lost or destroyed by increasing industrial and housing development.

The archaeologist looks at maps and written records with a critical eye. Human beings have basic needs that have to be satisfied. The archaeologist must try to look for sites from the point of view of early human beings, who were trying to provide for these needs.

WATER All cultures need a supply of fresh water. Most early cultures would not have been able to store fresh water in large amounts. These cultures had to either live near a water source or have a means of bringing water to them. Streams, rivers, and lakes were also an important means of transportation between villges and hunting grounds, and served as natural highways.

The archaeologist looks for clues on special maps that show the location not only of present-day rivers and lakes but also of valleys and other land depressions where a river or lake may once have existed. Maps that show surface features such as rivers, valleys, hills, roads, and bridges are called topographical maps.

FOOD People must eat. Many early groups depended on hunting and gathering to supply their food needs. During the spring and summer, groups of people, such as the Algonkin Indians of Vermont, camped together along the shores of lakes and major rivers. There they hunted, fished, and grew some vegetables. After the harvest, groups broke up and moved to the mountains to hunt the moose, deer, bear, and muskrat for the winter. Archaeologists look for evidence of early tribal groups along river banks and lake shores as well as along well established and very old footpaths in the mountains.

People who lived near large bodies of water often ate great numbers of shellfish. Piles of shells are a good indication that other artifacts will be found close by. Along the seacoast early tribes often tried to settle near bays where the tribes could fish in a protected area. Places where fresh water runs into the ocean are other logical places to hunt for signs of human activity. Those who depended on farming for food looked for rich land, easily cleared. Clues to farming settlements can be found in the soil. Soil layers rich in the remains of domesticated plants and animals can sometimes be identified by soil tests or by the seeds and pollen grains taken in soil samples. You'll learn more about the clues from the soil later in the section on the soil scientist.

Poor farming practices have made some once-rich farm lands difficult to identify because the rich topsoil layer has eroded. In the area known as the American Dust Bowl, about 100 million acres of the Great Plains had been blown away by the early 1930s because of drought, overplanting, and mismanagement. Only by strict conservation practices has some of this land been reclaimed.

DEFENSE People need to be safe. Commonly sites were chosen because they could be defended. Defense was important because in early times there were many dangers both from wild animals and from competing or warring groups of people. Often natural defenses were sought. A point of land protected by water or an area surrounded by mountains was desirable.

Other sorts of defenses were constructed. There were walls, sometimes around only a group of houses, sometimes around a whole city. The Great Wall of China defended the northern border of a whole country.

People also placed their houses and towns on high hills so that the townspeople could see an enemy from a long distance and have the advantage of shooting down on them. Another mark of a well-defended city was that food and water was available within the walls so that the city could withstand a long siege.

3. Water for the Cities

Where water was not readily available, ways were invented to bring the water closer. There are many examples of channeling water in many areas of the world. Perhaps the best known method is the aqueduct. Aqueducts were tunnels or pipelines constructed to transport water over long distances.

One of the best known of the early aqueducts was built by King Hezekiah 700 years before the birth of Christ. This aqueduct was built to supply Jerusalem with water. Cut through solid rock, the tunnel traveled about a third of a mile to bring water from a spring to a reservoir in the city limits.

The Assyrians built an aqueduct at about the same time to supply water to the city of Nineveh. This aqueduct was fifty miles long and utilized tunnels and open canals. At one part of the aqueduct the water on the way to the city passed over a 900-foot-long bridge that spanned a valley. About two million blocks of heavy limestone were used in the construction of this incredible bridge.

The best of the early aqueduct builders were the Romans. An estimated 260 miles of aqueducts supplied thirty-eight million gallons of water per day to the citizens of Rome.

4. The Great Wall of China

One of the most incredible attempts to defend an area by the use of walls is the Great Wall of China. The Chinese built the wall as a defense against sudden raids by Turkish and Mongol tribes. Made of stone and earth with a brick front, the original wall was twenty to thirty feet high and ten to thirteen feet wide with watch towers at intervals along its 450 mile length. A permanent northern army was formed to serve in this defense system, and additions to the wall increased its length to 1400 miles. Think of it: this was all built by hand more than two thousand years ago.

The Great Wall of China was one of the most incredible defence systems built by early man.

51

5. Search for a Lost City

Clues that lead an archaeologist to search an area range from tales told by elders to accounts of ancient communities found in old books and maps. For instance, Heinrich Schliemann's quest for the lost city of Troy began with his reading of Homer's epic poem, *The Iliad.*

As a young boy, Heinrich Schliemann was fascinated by the stories of Troy and its heroes. He became obsessed with someday locating the ancient city. All his energies were poured into getting enough money to finance his search.

He started as an errand boy, became a clerk, and taught himself eight languages. He worked his way up the business ladder step by step until, while still quite young, he had amassed a fortune. Finally at age forty-eight he began his Troy adventure.

Schliemann began digging in Turkey at a plateau called Hissarlik. Homer's *Iliad* provided clues. Troy was located on a hill from which the Trojans could easily see the Aegean seacoast, a place called the Hellespont. A great river flowed between the seacoast and Troy. Homer mentions two springs near the city. Schliemann was sure Hissarlik was the site; every detail seemed to match Homer's description of Troy's location.

No less than nine cities had been built on the plateau at Hissarlik. The earliest and deepest city was of the Bronze age. The second city (Troy II) burned to the ground. It was Troy III that Schliemann first believed to be the Troy of the *Iliad*. Later he changed his opinion to the second city, called the Burnt City. In the 1930s excavators finally decided that Troy VII-A was the true Troy written about by Homer. All in all, archaeologists have discovered that the site of Troy has had forty-six different building periods since its beginning. Nine cities had each been rebuilt repeatedly as earthquake, fire, and attack destroyed them one by one.

Schliemann dug into the hill, known as Hessarlik, and found not one, but nine cities had been built one upon the other.

6. A Good Site Is Used Again

Sometimes if a city or village had been built on an especially
good site with plenty of water and food, and easy defense, the

site was used over and over again. In many places in the Near East there are sites of this type that look like great mounds of earth. These are called *tells*, places where city has been built upon city.

Some of these tells were formed over many thousands of years. As the clay bricks of the buildings eroded from the action of wind and rain, and as dirt and dust piled up in the streets, the houses seemed to sink into the ground. Sometimes wooden buildings burned down. Then the people had to build them again. Often the builders leveled the old foundation, filled it level with the street, and built right on top of the old foundation. In this manner, the ground level grew higher and higher as time passed.

At other times, the people of a city were attacked and beaten by some enemy. The enemy might be an army from another land or a terrible disease. The people were wiped out. Perhaps the city was empty for a hundred years or more, but in time some people came along and saw that this was a perfect place to build for the same reasons that earlier people had built there. Only now the tell was even higher and therefore better for defense. This process continued until some tells contained the remains of more than twenty different communities.

When archaeologists dig into a tell, they find layers, called strata. Each stratum or single layer contains the artifacts from a time period when a particular group of people lived on the tell. Usually the deeper the artifacts are found, the older they are because as the ground level grew higher, later artifacts were piled on top of ones already there.

Archaeologists study these strata very carefully. Often when new groups began to build on a tell, they dug into the ground to build the foundations for their houses, and threw up dirt and artifacts that belonged in the next layer down. Archaeologists who dig these sites hundreds of years later find a mixing of materials from different layers and must work thoughtfully to figure out what this mixing means and how it happened.

7. Where to Dig

Once the archaeologist had located a promising site, there remains the question of where on the site to begin. Some sites may be quite large. Most artifacts are hidden underground. To dig an entire area could be time-consuming and might yield nothing.

How is the "where to dig" question answered?

First before an archaeologist places a foot on someone's land, the owner's permission to look around is requested.

Asking permission is important equally for the professional archaeologist and for the amateur. Bad feelings toward archaeology could easily be created by ignoring this simple but important rule.

The archaeologist looks at the suspected site from every possible angle.

FROM THE GROUND On foot the archaeologist covers the ground and looks for any artifacts that may be showing on the surface. Broken pieces of pottery, arrowheads, shell mounds, or fragments of worked stone or metal may provide the first clue to a backyard trash pit or village work area. Large stones, laid out in a pattern, may be the remains of a building foundation or an old well that has been filled in over the years. Sometimes the clue will be a mound of earth that is out of place in an otherwise flat area.

FROM THE AIR Evidence of human settlement may not be lying out in the open. If possible, the archaeologist will try to get some clues by flying over and looking down on the possible site. From the air, certain features are apparent that are not noticeable from the ground.

Crop marks Filled-in places, such as trash pits or cellar holes, provide rich soil. From an airplane or balloon, crops appear to grow thicker and have a darker color above such areas. In contrast, crops growing over areas where there is a buried wall or foundation tend to appear thinner and lighter in color.

Shadow marks Best seen from high places in the late afternoon or early morning when the sun is low, shadows are caused by places where the earth has fallen in on constructed irrigation systems or drainage ditches.

UNDER THE GROUND More clues can be discovered by searching under the soil. Sometimes the archaeologist forces a solid steel rod into the ground, a process called "probing." Walls and foundations hidden below the surface are hard. They stop the probe from being pushed through the soil. When a hard object is struck, probing all around the object provides evidence as to whether the object is alone or may be one of many that form a pattern, such as a straight line for a foundation or a circle for a well.

Probing with a steel tube instead of a rod is called "coring." By pushing the metal tube into the ground, the archaeologist brings up a core, or sample of the soil. This sample is carefully removed from the tube and studied to discover information about the soil layers. Coring sometimes turns up clues like coal or charcoal. This clue might lead the archaeologist to dig the site to find evidence of a campfire — and perhaps artifacts of the group that built the fire.

The archaeologist may try using a metal detector to find evidence of pipes, coins, nails, and other metal objects under the ground. These metal objects may be scattered artifacts or scraps that form a pattern where perhaps an old metal plow was left to corrode or where a wagon wheel fell apart, decayed, and left only the metal rods and nails.

Aerial views of a site taken from different heights help the archaeologist to study how the land was used and laid out.

8. Dowsing for Metal

Some people believe that underground metal can be located by a very old method known as "dowsing." You may have heard of people who locate water by holding a forked stick. When the dowser passes over underground water, the tip of the stick dips and points to the spot where the water can be found. Metal dowsing works much the same way except that the forked stick is replaced by a pair of bent wire rods.

Some dowsers claim that only a very few people can make dowsing rods work properly. Here is an opportunity to see if you are one of these few. Or is dowsing just a folk tale?

Cut two pieces of clothes hanger wire, each about two feet long. Make a right-angle bend in each, eight inches from one end. Hold the wires very lightly, one in each hand, with the bend resting on the forefinger. The short end of the wire should hang down through the closed fists. The knuckles of one hand should be touching the knuckles of the other hand. The wires, sticking out in front like the barrels of two guns, should be about two inches apart along their whole length (see illustration).

Walk very slowly over the area to be searched. Where metal is present under the ground, the two metal rods will cross. Some metal dowsers claim that their wires do not cross, but rather open wide over places where metal is to be found.

Treat dowsing as a theory to be proven or disproven. Think up clever ways of testing dowsing. How many people will you have to test to prove or disprove it to yourself?

A final cuation: watch out for parked cars and overhead electrical wires. These, too, can cause your wires to cross.

Bent clothes hangers make fine metal dowsing rods.

9. Conservation Archaeology — To Dig or Not to Dig

Suppose your research leads you to a place in town. You have spoken to the owner of the property, explained your interest, and received permission to take a look. Further suppose that using some of the clues to identifying a site, you have identified an area that looks as though it might contain some interesting and valuable information. Do you immediately grab a shovel and start digging? The answer is "No."

Archaeological sites are nonrenewable resources. Once destroyed, they can never be put back the same way. Much information has been lost or destroyed by well-meaning amateurs digging up a site. Archaeologists are experts trained to know what to look for. You are not. Does this mean that you cannot do any actual digging yourself? Not at all! But you must be willing to go through a few steps to ensure that you do not destroy information that might be historically valuable and irreplaceable. Here are the steps you should go through.

1. Consult the landowner. Explain your interest and what you want to do. If he or she does not want you to dig on the property, you might as well look elsewhere.
2. Go to the town library or historical society and find out whatever you can about the site. Talk to people who might know something about the site.
3. Get an adult to sponsor you, that is, someone to help you with questions you might have.
4. Write a letter to the state archaeologist's office to describe what you have found out and why you are interested in this site. (You'll find addresses for the state archaeologists in Appendix II in the back of this book.) Explain carefully the clues that lead you to believe that this site has histori-

cal significance. Ask for advice on whether to go ahead with your dig. It is just possible that the state archaeologist will ask you to hold off on your excavation until someone from the archaeologist's office can look at the site.

State archaeologists all over the United States are practicing a new brand of archaeology called conservation archaeology. This practice locates and preserves archaeological sites. By locating these sites ahead of time, state archaeologists are able to see that these sites are protected until they can be properly excavated by experts. This is a very important part of archaeology. If a site that you report comes under the protection of this agency, you can be proud to have contributed to this very important work of conservation.

5. Should you get the go-ahead from the state archaeologist, be sure to read the rest of this book before proceeding. You must now learn the steps of excavation and of complete record keeping, perhaps the most important lesson.

6. One final caution. Do not in any circumstances start a dig without planning to finish it. Any square you begin to excavate should be dug all the way down to where the soil is free of any evidence of human activity. In the following sections you'll learn more about the time necessary to dig.

Asking permission of the landowner, before exploring a site, is important.

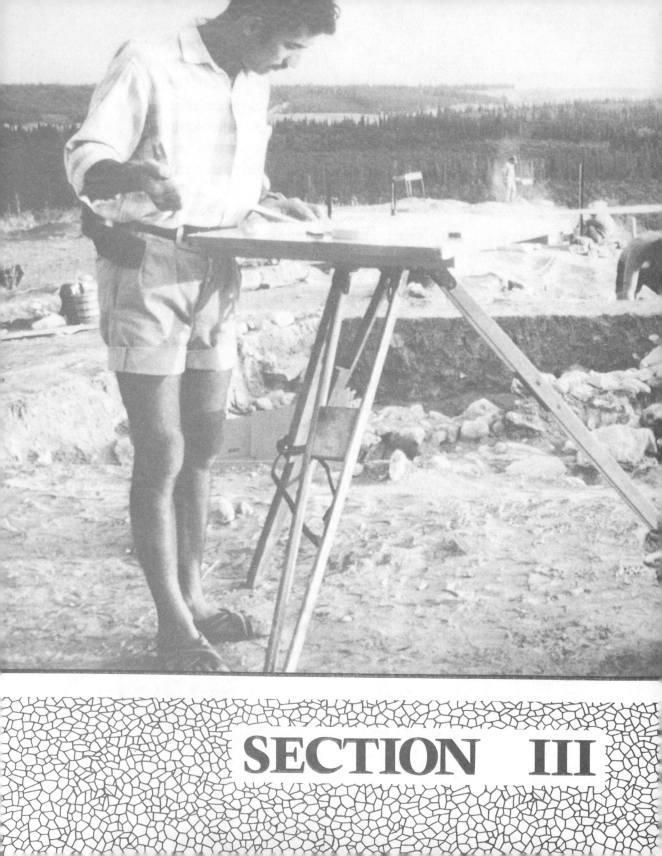

SECTION III

THE DIG

1. Prepare to Dig

Once the initial dig areas have been located, several things must be done before the actual *excavation*, digging, begins. The **64** areas must be mapped, archaeological squares must be marked, and serious research into the area's past must be pursued through every available resource.

MAPPING Mapping of an archaeological site is done by a surveyor. This is a person who measures the size, shape, position, and boundaries of the site for the archaeologist. From all of the measurements the surveyor makes up an official map to scale.

The site map, like the topographical map mentioned earlier, shows all of the surface features of the site: hills and valleys, streams, buildings and foundations, and roads. The official map can answer questions like these:

How high above sea level is the site?
What are the north, south, east, and west boundaries of the site?
How is the site located in relation to land that surrounds it?
Where will each square be located?

The surveyor lays a grid over the map. A grid is a pattern of lines like that found on graph paper. Laying a grid over the entire map and numbering each square in the grid make it possible quickly to find any area on the map. This grid is valuable to the archaeologist and others concerned with the dig because a grid provides common reference points for whatever area is being discussed.

At the dig site, a stake is driven into the ground at each corner of a grid square until the whole area is marked off in squares just as on the map.

Maps are important to the archaeologist. They are the tools that allow smooth communication at a dig site. Imagine trying to put together information after a dig is over without having a clear map to locate where artifacts were dug up. The archaeologist uses the map to help plan the next areas to be excavated. Finally maps help people who are reading about the dig to identify its location and to understand the archaeologist's conclusions. **65**

2. Mapping

Here is part of a site map for a nineteenth century tavern. The tavern is being studied by archaeologists before it is disassembled to be rebuilt at a museum. The tavern is the large shaded figure in the southeast quarter of this map. You can also see areas, marked by crosshatching, where the archaeologists are digging (such as in southeast quadrant 12, next to the tavern).

Grids also give you a sense of the size of objects and their distance from each other. If each square of this grid is two feet long by two feet wide, how big is the stove in the illustration? How far is it from the west wall to the east wall in this room?

You can make your own grid like this one, or use graph paper to make a scale drawing of a room in your house. You should measure and show the outline of the room. Use a compass to find out in which direction the room is facing and show direction on your drawing with a north arrow. Plot each piece of furniture exactly to scale and position each in its exact location in the room. Try this activity outside by drawing your yard and its contents.

Topographical map shows the elevation of the land, its valleys and hills.
TELL EL-HESI is in the bottom right-hand corner. You can tell that the east
side is steepest because the contour lines are closest together. **67**

3. Staking Out the Grid

In any location where the archaeologist has decided to dig, stakes are driven into the ground in the exact locations shown on the map. The stakes are connected by string making a pattern of squares over the entire area to be investigated. Each stake is given an identification number. A lot of care is taken to make these squares exact. When the excavation begins, it will become important to be able to locate the position of artifacts in these squares.

The size of the squares is decided before the map is drawn. For intance, the archaeologist might decide to use five-meter squares for digging the site of an Indian village. All the squares would then be made five meters wide by five meters long. Within this standard square, the archaeologist might decide to dig only a trench one meter long by five meters wide. Often if the archaeologist is unsure of a square's potential, a smaller area will be dug within the standard square. These "probe trenches" are used to discover information about the strata through which the crew will be digging. Sometimes the probe trenches yield information about the kinds of artifacts the diggers might hope to find in a particular area.

At times the dirt in a square will yield no artifacts and little information can be gained from studying the layers. In this case, the archaeologist will probably abandon the square. If, on the other hand, the yield from a particular square is high, the archaeologist may decide to dig a square directly beside the first. When this decision is made, the archaeologist is careful to leave a dirt wall, called a *balk*, between the two squares so that the artifacts from one square can be identified separately from those of the second square. Eventually the balk will be excavated also, but not until the archaeologist is sure that no confusion can arise from tearing down this wall.

At the site, areas to be dug are staked out with a balk left between adjacent squares.

4. Researching a Site

The archaeologist and other members of the dig team are constantly researching any written records dealing with their site and its history. Many documents can be valuable to an archaeologist studying recent sites. Let's take as an example a site from the early 1800s in New England. What are some of the resources that the archaeologist might find useful?

Maps, including old military maps, county records, insurance records, court records, and tax records all deal with land use and boundaries. These records can also provide clues about when property changed hands and what kinds of buildings were on the property.

Builders' ledgers and inventories kept by businessmen list artifacts that the archaeologist might expect to find as well as some of the sources of these artifacts.

Cemeteries may provide information about former owners of a site. Sometimes a grave inscription, called an epitaph, will even tell you what the person died from. Many early gravestones were made from local materials, and may tell you something of the local geology.

Early newspapers describe issues important to settlers as well as current events of the period.

Pictures, painted by artists of the period, provide insight into some of the styles and customs.

Private accounts, from such sources as letters, diaries, and personal account books, offer specific information about the period. They often talk about habits, practices, and materials that were important in the daily lives of people. This information is exactly the kind of thing the archaeologist is trying to reconstruct.

A collection of the designs used on early grave stones can be made by rubbing crayon or black wax across a piece of thin paper held tightly against the stone's design. (Get permission from cemetery officials before attempting.)

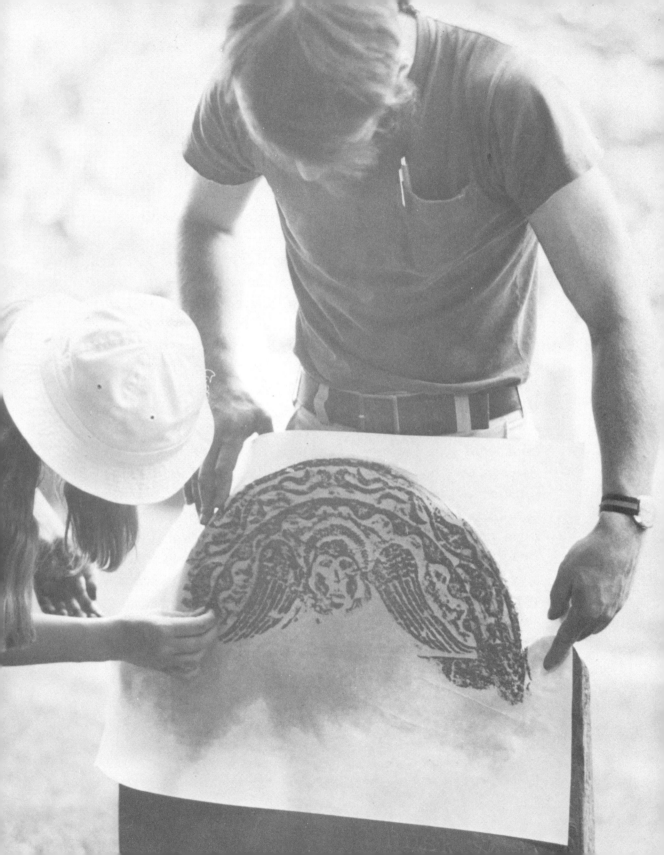

5. A Letter

Following is an excerpt from a twelve-year-old girl's letter to her mother. Lucy Goodale is writing from a boarding school in Massachusetts in 1832. From her short description of a day at school what can you learn about the period in which she lived?

[Wayland] Wednesday, May 30 [1832]

My dear Mother,

Thursday. *I have been to school today & found it so very pleasant that I must tell you a little about it, yet as it is nearly dark I cannot write long, but must be very concise in what I have to say. The school consists of about 30 young ladies, the oldest is Dea. Rice's daughter Abby. Miss Gleason opens the school by reading a few verses from the Bible & then she rings a little bell, when all the scholars immediately bend forward & lay their faces upon the bench, & she leads in prayer. After this we read in the Testament one verse apiece & then close our books and she questions us about what we have been reading. After this we have 2 or 3 minutes to whisper & she says we must think of all we want to say. We have this permission after reading in the afternoon after reading & at night all those who have made any communication except at this time, by signs or by writing must rise. If it is very necessary indeed for us to speak, we must hold up our hand & she will ask us what we want. If we are tardy we have neither the long nor the short recess. Always when a class is to recite she rings the bell, although they generally immediately succeed each other. Thus every thing goes on with the greatest order & regularity & I have been thus particular that you might see this.*

A detail from Lucy Goodale's letter showing her handwriting.

Thursday. I have been to school to day & fou[nd]
you a little about it, yet as it is nearly dark I can[not]
what I have to say. The school consists of about [?]
Abby. Miss Gleason opens the school by reading a few
little bell, when all the scholars immediately bend
she leads in prayer After this we read in the Testa[ment]
and she questions us about what we have been reading.
she says we must think of all we want to say. We h[ave]
afternoon after reading & at night all those who ha[ve]
this time, ~~thinkst vigas~~ or by writing must rise. If it
must hold up our hand & she will ask us what we
the long nor the short recess. Always when a class is
nerally immediately succeed each other. Thus every
[?] [?] these particulars that you ma[y]

6. Diary

Here is a section taken from a farmer's work and weather diary. From these entries made in 1831 what can you learn about Daniel Grant's life on his New Hampshire farm? His spelling has been used here.

MARCH

Wed 9	Cuting wood AM Town Meeting Clouday
Thurs 10	Cuting wood fair and cold
Fr 11	Cuting wood Chanel clear of Ice fair and warm
Sat 12	Cuting wood warm rainy
Sun 13	very warm and pleasant
Mon 14	Spliting wood cold and windy
Tue 15	Spliting wood warm and pleasant
Wed 16	Cuting boards warm and clouday
Thurs 17	To work at the door cold and clouday
Fr 18	CF clear and cold froze arond the shore

APRIL

Sat 2	fencing fair and cold for the season
Sun 3	fair and pleasant wind east
Mon 4	ploughing cool and clouday
Tue 5	CF Great Rain
Wed 6	Sowing (Rie?) and fencing fair and cool
Thurs 7	fast fair and very warm
Fr 8	CF cold and rainy
Sat 9	CF cold and the Greatest wind for many years
Sun 10	Cold and winday Ice nearly half inch thick
Mon 11	Halling manure rainy
Tue 12	CF Snowed 2 inches cold and winday
Wed 13	Halling wood for Jones fair and cold
Thurs 14	Went to Epping for poles fair and warm
Fr 15	ploughing fair and warm
Sat 16	to work about home rainy day
Sun 17	very rainy freshet hiest that been this year

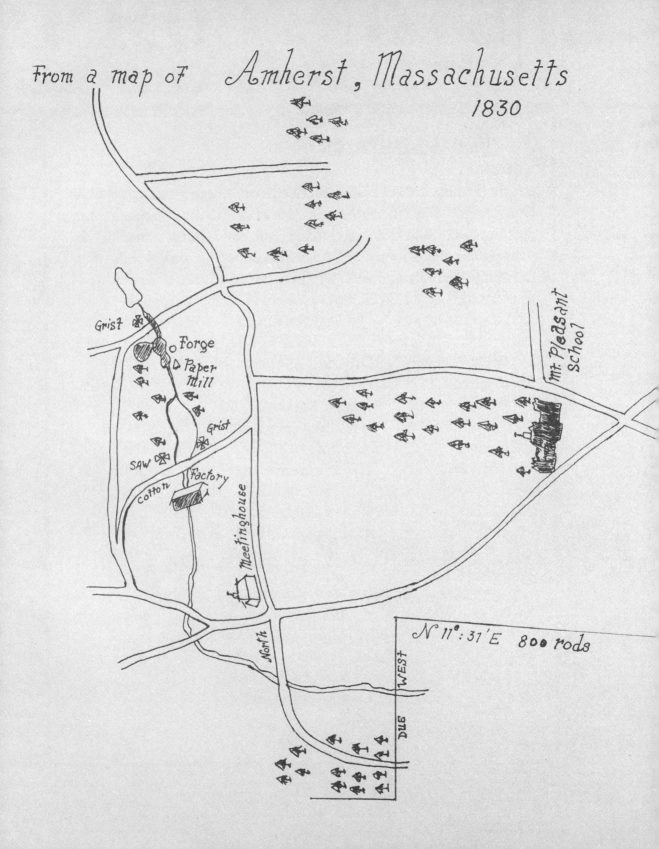

From a map of *Amherst, Massachusetts* 1830

Grist

Forge

Paper Mill

Grist

SAW

Cotton Factory

Meetinghouse

North

Mt. Pleasant School

DUE WEST

N 11°:31'E 800 rods

7. Newspapers

Following are several advertisements taken from the *Boston Commercial Gazette and Daily Morning Advertiser*, dated Monday, June 30, 1828. Advertisements tell you what kinds of products were being sold by various companies and what kinds of raw materials were being used. What do the addresses of the companies listed below suggest to you about the city of Boston?

16,000 LBS.

Spanish Block Tin, for sale by Munson & Barnard, 17 Central-Wharf

BOTTLES

Porter and Wine-bottles, and all other kinds of Black and Green Glass Ware of the manufacture of the New England Glass Company, constantly for sale by TYLER & BINNEY, 33 Long-Wharf

8. What Changes Have Occurred in Your City or Town?

Most cities and towns have a historical society or other group interested in the history of the area. Sometimes a group of interested citizens meet to exchange information that they have uncovered about the town. You can find out about the historical society in your city or town and ask to look through their collections of documents. Sometimes a lot of this information is housed in the local library.

Compare old maps and photographs of your area with those produced more recently. See if you can locate

buildings that are still standing after many years,
buildings that have disappeared or changed in appearance,
old roads that have changed direction or have fallen into disuse, and
streams or rivers that have changed course or disappeared.

On an old map find the location of the building you now live in. Before your house, was there anything on the same piece of property?

Often you can read about changes in your city or town. What was the main industry and where was it located? Is this still the leading industry? How did the early settlers of your area supply themselves with the necessities of water, shelter, food, and defense? How have our methods of supplying these needs changed over the years?

Fri 1	went after withins	Clear and Cool
Sat 2	fencing fair and Cold for the Searn	
Sun 3	fair and pleasant	wind East
Mon 4	ploughing Cool and Cloudey	
Tue 5	C F great Rain	
Wed 6	sowing Rie and fencing fair and Cool	
Thurs 7	fast fair and very warm	
Fri 8	C F Cold and Rainy	
Sat 9	C F Cold and the greatest wind for many y	
Sun 10	Cold and windey Ice nearly half Inch thick	
Mon 11	halling manure Rainy	
Tue 12	C F Snowed 2 Inches Cold and windey	
Wed 13	halling wood for Jones fair and Cold	
Thurs 14	went to Epping for poles fair and warm	
Fri 15	ploughing fair and warm	
Sat 16	to work about home Rainy day	
Sun 17	very Rainy freshet hiest that been this	
Mon 18	S M fair pleasant	
Tue 19	ploughing the Orchard warm and showery	
Wed 20	ploughing warm and showery	
Thurs 21	takeing down fence fair and Cold	
Fri 22	Fencing lower feild Cool	
Sat 23	Fencing Cold and Cloudey	
Sun 24	fair and pleasant	
Mon 25	fencing Cold and Cloudey	
Tue 26	fencing Cold and Cloudey	
Wed 27	ploughing for Rowe fair and Cold	
Thurs 28	C F very Cold Rain storm	
Fri 29	S m Cold and Rainy	
	C F Cool and Cloudey	

9. Oral History

Written records are not the only resources that can be used to obtain personal accounts of a period. If the site is recent enough or still in use, an elderly person living nearby might remember some of the details of the area's history. Information gathered through conversation is known as oral history and can be valuable for filling in details and adding to your understanding of the past.

From interviews with residents you can find out many things. What kinds of activities have taken place at the site over the years? What changes have occurred in the buildings and land? Who owned and worked the property and are there any anecdotes about them?

Choose an old house, store, or factory that you would like to know about. Ask around. Is there an elderly person who has lived in the area for years? Telephone this person and ask if you might interview him or her about the site that you are interested in. Prepare some questions ahead of time. Ask questions like these:

Has the site changed much in apearance over the years?
What was made or sold there?
How were goods picked up or delivered?
What raw materials were used? How were they prepared for use?
What were the steps to making the product? (One recent interviewer discovered the store she was researching carried ''everything'' — including false teeth!)

Going to your interview with a prepared list of questions will prevent embarrassing silences while you try to think of another question to ask, and will ensure that you get at least the information you came to get. Often you will find that you end up with far more information than you expected, a new friend, and some great stories from the past.

Use a notebook or a tape recorder to get your information correct. Bring a friend along; you'll be a lot less nervous. Don't forget to ask if there are others who might have information about your area of interest. Good research often opens up new areas to explore.

All of this background information is important, but the archaeologist must be careful not to rely too much on it. History, after all, is written by people; and each person views an event or a period according to his or her own experience. When personal experience colors the facts, the distortion is called prejudice. Prejudice may show up in descriptions even when people are trying to be totally honest and accurate. Nobody can see everything that is going on and remember it accurately.

The information dug up from the ground may disagree with information found in old documents. In the end it is the artifacts that the archaeologist must use to form the final report. It is the archaeologist's special prejudice to base his or her picture of the past on the information provided by clues excavated from the site. After the archaeologist has drawn conclusions from the data, that information will be compared with other sources. In this way, historical documents and archaeological findings complement each other.

Interviewing grandparents about an old site adds detail and color to research notes.

10. The Scientific Method

Archaeology had its beginnings in the form of treasure hunting. The people who practiced this early form were interested in finding and digging up valuable objects from the past. Often ancient peoples made religious articles and other ornaments out of precious metals and jewels. Many other objects, made of more common materials, were intricately carved or gracefully shaped. People admired them and wanted to own them.

Doors were broken down and burial places raided for these "art treasures." Because people will collect almost anything, artifacts, from arrowheads to bottles to the entire contents of ancient temples, were removed from their original placement by people who wished merely to own them. Thus countless irreplaceable artifacts were removed to private houses where they have been handsomely displayed — but never to the public at large.

Other people were interested only in the money that these artifacts would bring if dismantled and melted down for the precious materials of which they were made. This destruction is unfortunately still going on today because some people are insensitive to the valuable information that they are destroying.

Eventually it was realized that archaeology could provide the key to uncovering information about the past, information that was available in no other way. Archaeologists learned to slow down digs and record everything, whether a simple bone or a golden goblet, before it was removed from the ground. The treasures are still found, and they are still just as valuable. It just takes a little longer to reach them through scientific excavation; and the rewards are increased many fold.

11. Tomb Robberies

It was a triumph for Howard Carter and the Earl of Carnarvon as they descended the sixteen stairs that would take them to the entrance of King Tutankhamen's tomb. They had spent six seasons searching for it in the Valley of the Kings in Egypt. There, on the lower part of the doorway, was the seal of Tutankhamen. But what was this! The seal of the necropolis officials, the guards of the tombs, was not placed on the original plaster. The tomb had been entered by thieves and had had to be reclosed by the necropolis guards.

Their find turned out well for Carter and Carnarvon. The tomb had been robbed twice, but the thieves had been discovered quickly each time. The first time the thieves made off with objects made of gold, silver, and bronze. The necropolis officials discovered the entry and filled the corridor between the outside and inside doors with sand and rock. The second group of robbers had to tunnel through the rubble to get in. This time they were after the costly oils stored in large alabaster jars. Because the jars would not fit through the narrow tunnel, the thieves had to empty the oils into waterskins. The archaeologists discovered a finger mark, probably that of a thief, on the inside of one of the jars. The mark had been preserved in the thick, oily liquid for centuries. Again the robberies had been discovered quickly and the tomb resealed.

Unlike other objects stolen in tomb robberies in the Valley of the Kings, almost all of Tutankhamen's tomb treasures were left untouched. Many mummies of kings had been discovered, but only Tutankhamen was in his original tomb and had all of his burial treasures intact. Almost all of his tomb equipment and personal possessions were found. At last archaeologists were able to see just how an Egyptian Pharaoh was buried.

84 *The antechamber of King Tut's tomb was hastily put back in order by necropolis officials before it was resealed.*

12. Excavating a Square

Let's imagine that you are the archaeologist beginning the excavation of a new square. The site has been surveyed, mapped, and marked with stakes. You have chosen the spot where you want to begin, and you have stretched string between the four corner stakes to outline a square.

First you search the grass in the square looking for any artifacts that are showing on the surface. Aha! You find a broken piece of pottery. (Archaeologists call these pieces sherds.) The sherd is placed in a plastic bag and labeled with the square location and a note that it was found in the grass. You begin to remove the turf. It is cut into squares and lifted carefully as you check for artifacts. The turf sections are moved away to be replaced after the dig is completed.

Next you make a top plan of the square. This is a drawing of any large rocks, pieces of wood, or artifacts showing in the square. A top plan is made before the dig begins each morning and is used during the day to note the position of any artifacts that the archaeologist feels worthy of note. Now you are ready to begin digging.

The watchword now is "slowly." Each artifact must be dug from its location with care. The artifact must not be destroyed. Each artifact is treated as if it held a valuable clue. It must not even be moved until all the information that its location can provide has been recorded.

If the archaeologists have dug a probe trench and have determined that no artifacts are likely to be found above two feet down, the archaeologists might begin carefully digging with a shovel until they are close to the two-foot level. At the first sign of an artifact before that level, they would immediately stop shoveling and begin using one of the smaller tools.

A small spoon is the tool used for carefully removing dirt from between the bones without disturbing their placement.

13. Tools of the Archaeologist

A *patish,* or hand pick, is used for loosening the soil before it is scraped into a pile with a trowel, like those masons use for laying brick. The loose dirt scraped up by the trowel is brushed into a dustpan and emptied into a labeled bucket. When artifacts are discovered, small tools, such as dental picks and paint brushes, are gently used to clean off dirt. This cleaning is done without moving the artifacts from their location.

Not every artifact is worthy of being measured, drawn, photographed, and cleaned *in situ,* in place. Small broken bits of glass, bone, leather, and sherds are so common and so scattered throughout a dig site that their exact position is not recorded. They are, however, separated according to the material of which they are made, and their general location is noted.

Every bit of soil is placed in baskets or buckets and brought to yet another of the archaeologist's tools, the sifter. The dirt from each labeled bucket is loaded onto a framed screen, which is then shaken to send the dirt through the small, quarter-inch holes. What is left on the screen are stones and in many cases figurines, beads, bones, teeth, and bits of glass and pottery so small that they were overlooked by the diggers in the pits. The artifacts found by sifting are given back to the digger whose bucket was sifted and are placed in his or her artifact bags.

Sometimes if the soil is very wet and clumped together, the dirt will be subjected to wet screening instead of sifting. Wet screening is a technique in which dirt is placed in a bucket with a screen bottom. The bucket is dunked up and down in a barrel of water until all the dirt is washed away through the screen. Small artifacts missed in digging can be spotted this way.

Flotation is another process that uses water — and the same bucket. This time you are looking for anything that floats to the top of the water during the slow up and down motion used to wash the dirt away. Many organic materials, such as seeds and small bones, will float. The top of the water is skimmed, using a net as fine as a nylon stocking; and all of the organic material is placed in a properly labeled bag.

14. Tagging the Artifacts

The diggers slowly work their way through each layer of dirt. Any artifacts that are small and fairly common are carefully removed from the soil and placed in properly labeled plastic bags. Each bag is labeled with the following information:

1. The material of which the object is made (such as metal, ceramic, bone, plant tissue, or glass).
2. Location of the square.
3. Locus number — A locus number is a number assigned to identify a place of special importance to the archaeologist. For example, a locus number would be assigned for a change in soil color or for the discovery place of some important artifact that might be significant for dating purposes. Whenever a new locus is found, it is drawn on the top plan, its location is measured, and a soil sample is taken.
4. Lot number — A lot number is a number assigned to each basket or bucket being filled so that the baskets or buckets don't become confused.
5. Initials of the person doing the digging.
6. The date.

The artifact tag has information about what the artifact is, as well as when and where it was found.

15. Important Artifacts

If an artifact looks as though it might be important, the archaeologist goes through a few extra steps to ensure that all of the information will be saved. Important artifacts would include burial objects, any tool or weapon, an artifact with identification marks that might make it easy to date, or a concentration of artifacts that should not be moved until their relationships to each other can be studied.

Important artifacts are carefully cleaned using dental picks and small brushes. The artifacts are measured and drawn on the top plan made that morning. A depth reading is taken to show exactly how far down the artifact was found. All of the information is recorded in the archaeologist's field notebook. Finally a photograph is taken for later study and as proof that the object was found as stated. Again the archaeologist takes good care of these objects because there is only one chance to note the original position and condition of the objects and their relationship to each other and to the soil layers. Once the artifacts are moved, they are out of place forever.

All objects go to the field laboratory to be processed. There at least part of each day is devoted to the activities of cleaning, cataloging, and storing artifacts that have come out of the ground that day. Many of the artifacts will be measured and weighed. Many of them will have their location written on them in India ink. All will be examined by the archaeologist before they are sent to various experts for analysis.

The archaeologist makes a preliminary reading of the artifacts each day in order to discover patterns emerging in the squares. A section of pipe found in one square, the leftover foundation of a well in another square, and evidence of a drainage ditch in a third square may lead the archaeologist to dig other squares in the hope of discovering how these finds were used together. Studying top plans and artifacts helps the archaeologist form a picture of where the best information is being found.

16. Chariot Burials

Chariot burials, like those found in northern France, illustrate why the archaeologist is careful not to move artifacts until their relationships to each other are shown.

In the village of Vix in northern France is a hill-fort where archaeologists unearthed a spectacular grave. In the center of the grave was the body of a thirty-year-old woman lying on a chariot-carriage. Stacked neatly to one side were the wheels, removed perhaps to signify that the chariot was no longer for worldly use.

An accurate reconstruction of the chariot was made possible because of the care taken by the archaeologists in their excavation. All of the parts of the decayed vehicle were noted and drawn as the archaeologists worked their way slowly through the dirt. They discovered that the chariot was four feet five inches long, rectangular, with a decorative brass balustrade and a fur-lined wooden back. The woman, a princess of the late Hallstatt group, probably sat in a half-reclining position. She was buried with richly jeweled bracelets on her wrists, a necklace of amber and diorite around her neck, and a golden diadem on her head.

In some of the chariot burials in China, the grave held even the bodies of horses in their proper place at the head of the chariot.

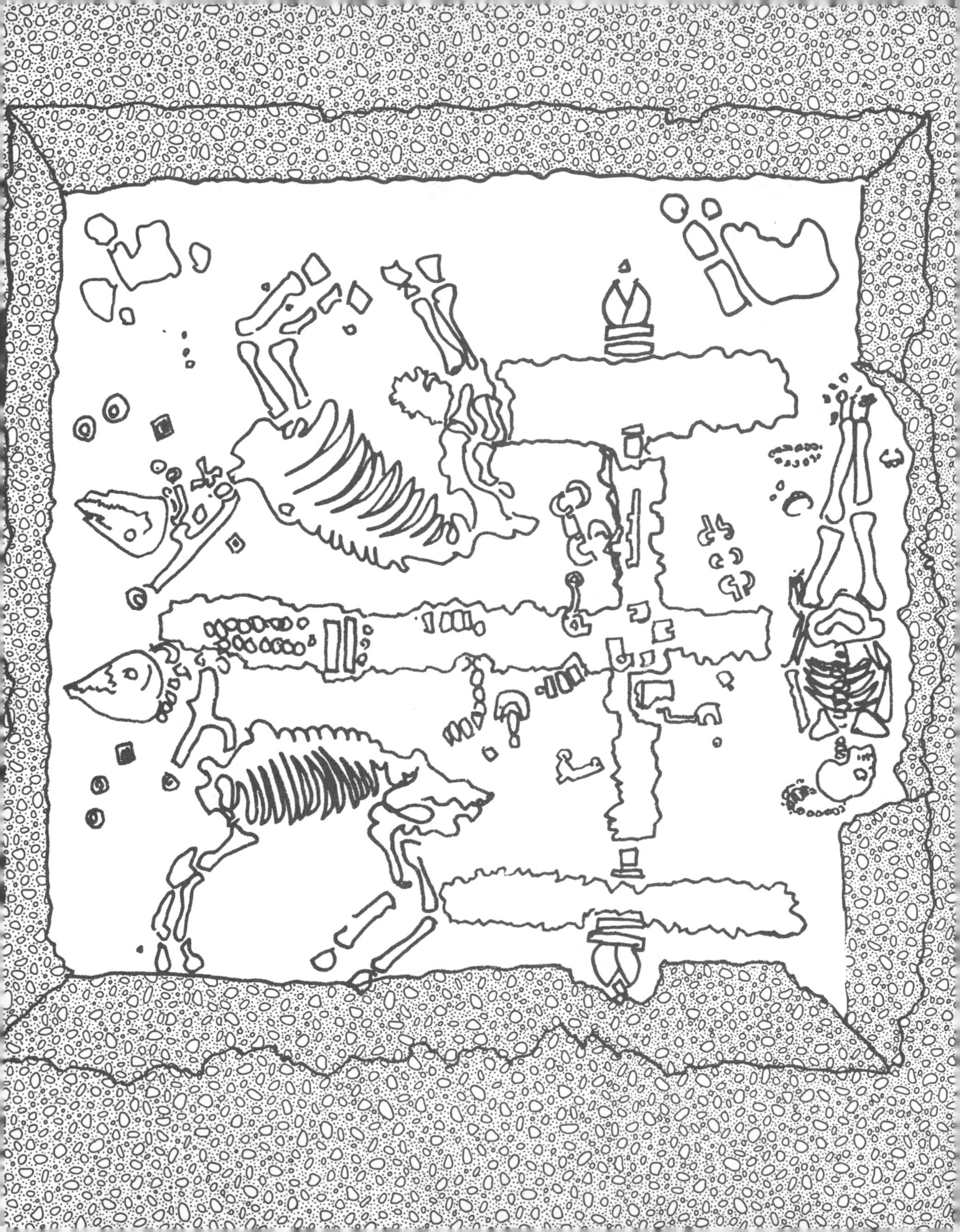

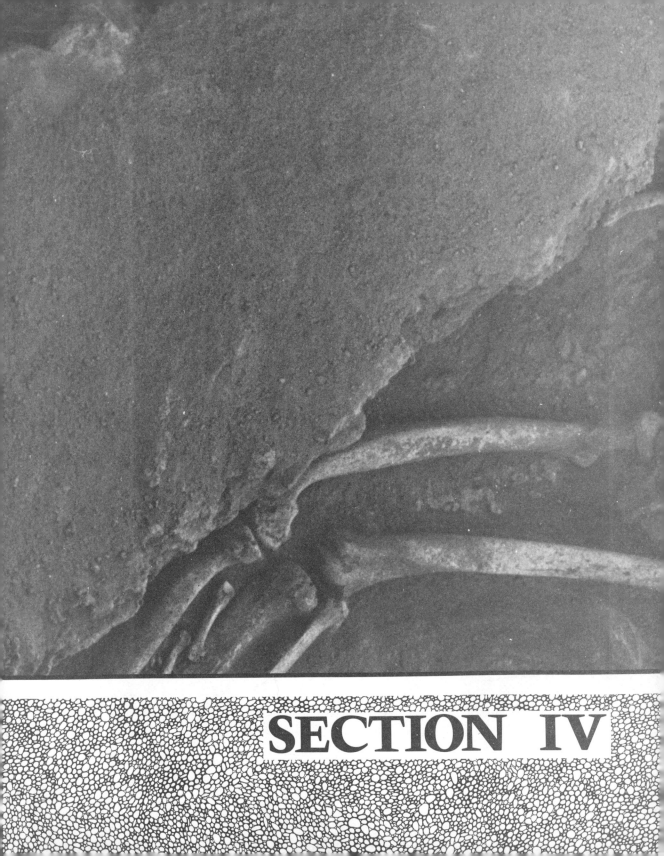

SECTION IV

SOLVING THE MYSTERY

1. The Experts

On a dig there are many experts who help the archaeologist get as much information as possible from the dirt. Some of these specialists are needed in the field almost every day. Among these are the artist, the photographer, and the soil scientist. Others, like the botanist, the zoologist and the epigrapher (an inscription expert) must work with special equipment or collections to analyze, test, and compare the artifacts. Much of this work is done in science laboratories and in museums with large collections of artifacts that can be used for comparisons.

The jobs of eleven different specialists are described in the pages that follow. Often the archaeologist will need every one of these experts to help on a dig. Each job description will include an activity or activities for you to do. These activities are like those the experts perform for the archaeologist. By working slowly through these activities, you can practice the skills needed by amateur and professional archaeologists. If one sort of job particularly interests you, you can find out more about it at your public library.

The microscope is an important tool for examining everything from the minute wear-patterns on rock to identifying species of pollen grains.

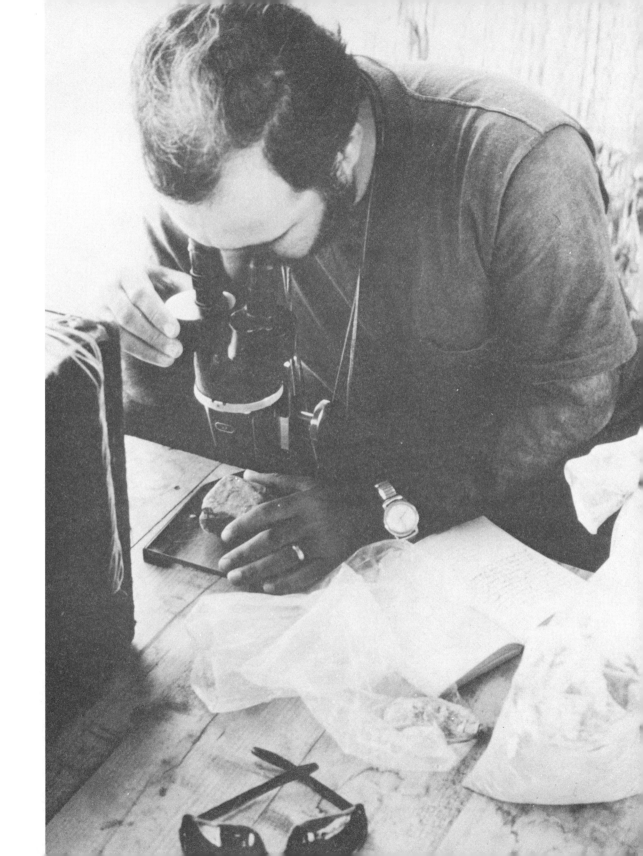

2. The Artist

The artist may be any digging crew member who has the ability to draw objects carefully to scale. The artist's job is to

make the top plan each day and to fill in newly found objects as the day progresses.

Balk drawings must be done carefully to ensure an accurate record of the strata. Accidents, such as balk walls collapsing under someone's weight, or natural disasters, such as walls being eroded by heavy rains, make it essential that these drawings are done regularly.

The most difficult part of the artist's job is drawing the objects and their relationships to each other exactly to scale. The artist must often reduce the drawings from life-size without changing the relative size of individual parts of the artifacts. This kind of drawing is usually done on graph paper. Just as you would on a map, you look at the drawings with the scale in mind.

The archaeological artist frequently cannot choose the angle from which the object must be drawn. In a top plan, for example, the drawing must be done from above, looking down on the square and its contents.

Try a top drawing of your own. Pick an object, such as a cup, vase, or piece of bone. Place the object on the ground and stand or sit directly above it. Measure it across in several places and write your measurements on a quick sketch of the object.

Take a piece of graph paper and decide on a scale to use for this drawing. Will each square of the graph paper equal an inch? A half inch? Now draw your object to scale on the graph paper.

Often objects drawn in this way are not recognizable from the drawing. The artist takes care of this problem by labeling the drawing or by identifying it with a number that is later explained in the field notebook.

The bank along a river is a good place to practice drawing soil layers. On your graph paper, draw to scale the strata that you observe along a riverbank. Measure the thickness of the layers and note them on your drawing. Label each soil layer by color or soil type (discussed in the section on the soil scientist). Don't neglect to draw the large rocks protruding from the soil.

101

3. The Photographer

The photographer is concerned with taking pictures of the artifacts so that they are recognizable and their location and size are shown in proper perspective. Often the photographer must get above the square so that the picture can be shot straight down on the artifacts. To show size, the photographs are taken with a scale, such as a meter stick or other object of known size, placed close to the artifact.

After artifacts have been cleaned and pieced together in the laboratory, the photographer will again take pictures of them as a record of what has been found at the site.

Lighting the artifacts properly when photographing them is one of the technical problems with which the photographer must deal. On location the light in the squares is often uneven or the artifacts are hidden in deep shadow. Sometimes an entire square must be shaded from the bright sun so that the picture can be taken without glare and bright spots, which obscure the details in the picture. In the laboratory, the photographer lights the objects with special floodlights. Moving the lights allows the artifacts to be photographed in detail without shadows or blurs.

If you have a camera, try photographing objects outdoors. Try to find ways to shade or light objects so that your pictures are lighted evenly and show as much detail on the objects as possible.

The photographer records the exact location of artifacts before they are moved. Note the use of the meter stick as a scale.

4. The Soil Scientist

The soil scientist's job is to help the archaeologist understand the story that the soil layers can tell. The soil scientist can offer expert opinion on many questions. How was the original soil layer laid down? Was the soil laid down by people's leveling the land or perhaps by a river or stream flooding its banks each year?

What can the chemical content of the soil tell us? A lot can be learned about the past uses of land through analysis of its chemical makeup. For instance, if a high concentration of phosphates is found, it is likely that agricultural activities took place in the area. Nitrates and phosphates in animal manure have been used for centuries to fertilize farm land. High phosphate content usually indicates concentrated human activity.

Sometimes the archaeologist may want to describe the soil in terms of its color. For instance, in parts of New England the second soil layer, called the *B horizon,* is normally a pale, sandy color. Discovery of a dark color might indicate an early campfire site. To describe the soil color in terms that other archaeologists will readily understand, the archaeologist uses a Munsell chart. This chart is known world-wide to geologists and archaeologists.

A sample of the soil from different levels can be taken using this soil auger.

It consists of a series of color chips, which are compared to dry soil samples. From this comparison a soil color number is assigned to each sample.

Another way that the soil scientist can describe the soil is in terms of the size of its particles. A simple soil classification system is given below. Use it the next time you go for a walk. Identify areas in your neighborhood where each of these particle sizes can be found. If some soils seem to fall into categories between these four basics, combine the terms to increase the usefulness of your chart. Collect samples of each of the soil sizes and label them to be used for comparison when you try a dig of your own. Indicate where you found each sample and under what conditions.

SOIL PARTICLE CHART

Sand	Very loose and made up of single grains that are easily separated. When moist, sand can be squeezed into a simple shape. The shape will crumble when touched.
Loam	Made up of different-sized particles of sand, silt, and clay. Loam is gritty but fairly smooth to the touch. When moist, loam will mold into a simple shape that can be carefully handled without falling apart.
Silt	A fine-grained soil that, when dry, feels soft when rubbed between the fingers. When very wet, this soil will make muddy puddles. When moist, silt can be squeezed between the fingers to make a ribbon that will break as it is made.
Clay	A very fine-grained soil. When wet, clay is sticky and can be molded into a variety of shapes. When dry, it will form hard clumps, which crumble when struck.

5. Soil Testing

One of the simpler chemical tests you can do on soil is the pH test. This identifies the amount of acid in the soil and indicates the types of plants that have grown in the area. For instance, soil tends to be more acidic under pine forests than under deciduous forests. (Deciduous trees are those that lose their leaves.)

The value of pH is measured on a scale from 0 to 14: 7 is neutral, neither acid nor alkaline; 0–6 is the acid range; 8–14 is the alkaline range. Most plants grow somewhere between 4 and 8.

Testing devices for pH are inexpensive to buy at any garden supply center or swimming pool dealer. One of the easiest devices to use is a chemically treated paper tape. The paper changes color to indicate the pH number.

To test your soil pH, first get a pint-size glass container, and a wooden or plastic spoon. Rinse the container with distilled water, available at supermarkets. Don't touch the inside of the container or you may contaminate your reading.

Place several spoonfuls of test soil in the container and cover the soil with one-half inch of distilled water. Carefully mix the contents with your spoon; then allow the soil to settle to the bottom and the water to clear. Holding only one end of the chemically treated paper, pull out a 2-inch strip. Dip the untouched end in the clear water over the soil. Remove the strip and compare it to the color chart on the side of the tape dispenser. The color match will show your pH number.

If you are interested in doing more of the kinds of tests that a soil scientist would do, Appendix I at the end of the book lists a test-kit address.

Linea and Heather are testing the pH of a soil sample. This sample came from under a pine tree and is very acid.

6. The Botanist

1.

2.

Botany is the study of plants. The botanist helps the archaeologist by identifying plants that were growing during past periods. The archaeologist is interested in the botanist's answers to several questions.

What kinds of plants were available as food sources? What nonfood plants were available? Sometimes our ancestors used plants for other purposes such as weaving, caning, rope making, and medicine.

Was the climate of the period similar to that of today? Plants that grow only in particular climatic conditions can provide clues to the climate of the period. As an example, maple trees wouldn't grow under desert conditions. If you discovered maple seeds in a desert dig, what possible explanations could you imagine for your find?

The male portion of a plant, the stamen, produces small, powderlike sex cells, called pollen. In many plants this pollen is carried to the female portion of the plant by wind. Much of the pollen never reaches its target and falls to the ground. This fall is known as pollen rain. The pollen grain for each type of plant is identifiable and different from the pollen grains of any other plant.

If a layer from a peat bog contains pollen only from pine and birch, the climate was fairly cold. Oak, elm, and other deciduous trees grow in more moderate climates.

The botanist often has to identify a plant from seeds collected in the flotation process, from pollen grains collected from

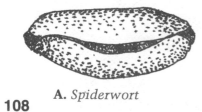

A. *Spiderwort*

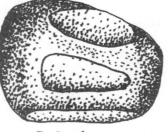

B. *Sorghum*

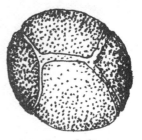

C. *Corydalis*

soil samples, or from fossil remains found in rock during the digging. Plant remains normally decay quickly. Seeds and pollen grains have a coating that can protect them for many years, and under the right conditions they fossilize very readily. Often they can still be identified after hundreds of years.

Unless the seed or pollen grain is familiar, the botanist must use an identification book or a *type collection* for help with identification.

A botanic type collection is a collection of types of plants or plant parts, such as pollen grains or seeds. In the illustration are two pollen grains (1 and 2) that need identification. Each pollen grain has a shape that is unique to its species. By using the pictured type collection (A–G) in the bottom illustration, you can identify the species of plant from which each pollen grain comes. Imagine how hard it must be to identify a particular pollen grain with a type collection that numbers in the hundreds or thousands!

Sometimes the ancient pollen grain is unlike any that has been thus identified. In that case, the botanist tries to identify the family from which the grain came and perhaps earns the honor of naming the new plant.

A botanist is able to identify trees by their seeds, pollen, bark, leaves, and flowers. Start a type collection of your own by collecting these parts from trees in your area. There are identification books to help you decide among the species. Afterwards you can use the flower-drying method described earlier in this book to dry the different parts of the tree. Then mount your collection on heavy paper or cardboard and you will have your own type collection.

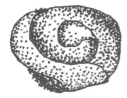

D. *Monkey Flower*

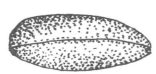

E. *Blue Gentian*

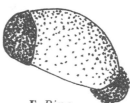

F. *Pine*

G. *Water Lily*

7. The Zoologist

Zoology is the study of animals. Like the botanist, the zoologist helps the archaeologist to identify species.

Early people had many uses for animals: food; leather for clothing, shelter, and lashing; and bone for tools, weapons, and ornaments. By knowing something of the habits of the animals used and hunted, the archaeologist can determine something of the habits of the hunters. If the animals were migratory, did people follow the animals' migratory routes or perhaps try to domesticate herds for use in a more permanent setting? Maybe the animals were eaten only during particular seasons of the year.

Much research has been done on early animal species and the ways they evolved through millions of years. Zoologists have used such sources as animal skeletons, cave paintings, written descriptions, and in a few rare cases even frozen or mummified remains.

Often the zoologist will have to make an identification with only a small bit of evidence, a bone or two or even just a small fragment of a bone.

In the illustration are skull fragments (1, 2, and 3) from three different species of animal. Use the animal skull type collection (A–F) to identify the animal to which each fragment belongs.

You can make your own bone type collection. Here are a few suggestions on where to find bones.

Butchers often remove bones from meat before selling it. A butcher will be able to tell you which bones you are getting and from what animal they come.

You can buy many foods like chicken and fish, with all the

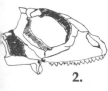

1.

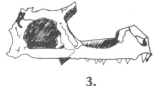

2.

3.

A. *Paleozoic Reptile 50.*   **B.** *Sea turtle 51.*

Chicken bones are easy to come by and make good skeletons.

bones. If no one at the supper table throws away any bones, you will have a complete skeleton. Remove the bones and place them in bleach overnight. In the morning, you will have a pile of snowy white bones.

Pet shops, mink farms, hunters, fishermen, and trappers are other good sources of animal skeletons.

You can keep your bones in labeled boxes or mount the bones on sheets of cardboard. Maybe you'd like to glue and wire your skeleton in a more natural position. Use a light wire or wood frame to help the skeleton stay in position.

C. *Sphenodon 52.*

D. *Iguana 53.*

E. *Python 54.*

F. *Early reptile, related to crocodilians 55.*

8. The Geologist

Geologists are scientists who sutdy rocks and minerals and the way the land was formed. Geologists may help the archaeologist form a picture of how the land took on the shape of mountains, valleys, or flatlands. Geologists also help the archaeologist to understand what kinds of rocks and minerals the early settlers had available as raw materials for building and for tool and weapon making.

A special kind of geologist, called a lithologist, studies stone and its uses. This scientist helps the archaeologist identify constructed stone tools and weapons, which often look like chipped and weathered stone. Sometimes it requires an expert to identify the difference between an artifact made by people and a stone altered by natural forces.

Archaeologists occasionally try to make some tool, weapon, or other artifact just as the ancient craftsman would have done, and to use the same tools and materials to do the job. This process, called experimental archaeology, helps the archaeologist to understand better a people's way of life and their basic skills. How much time and effort would it have taken to make a stone

Slate is difficult to shape but gives a sharp cutting edge.

ax blade? What kind of stone would chip or flake properly to make the most effectively sharpened blade or point? How was the tool used and what does its use tell us about the daily lives of the people who made it? These questions might be answered by experimental archaeology.

By looking through a microscope at how a stone implement has worn down, the archaeologist can tell much about its use. The archaeologist can figure out how the tool was held, the direction in which it moved, and the material it was used on.

You can study the wearing down process by carving a tool out of soap and then noticing how it wears. Cut a bar of soap in half lengthwise. Carve the end of one piece of the soap to look like a chisel blade. Carve the second piece of soap to a long, pointed shape like that of a child's thick pencil. Gently draw the beveled edge of your first piece of soap across a piece of leather or wood. Place the pointed tool between the palms of both hands, and twirl it gently into sand or gravel. Because soap is much softer than stone, the soap tools can give you a speeded-up view of how a harder material would wear after long use. Note the lines formed on the chisel head. These lines tell you that the tool was used for some kind of scraping activity. The circular lines on the pencil-shaped tool suggest its use.

Carve the soap to a chisel-like edge.

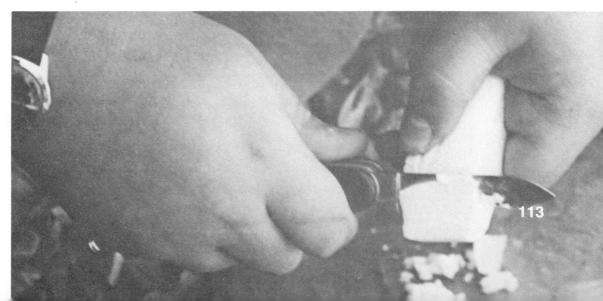

9. Experimental Archaeology — Dyeing

Archaeologists are interested in every phase of early life. They are interested in dyes because many peoples used dyes and paints made from natural materials. These dyes were used in personal art and for decorating cloth. On the opposite page is a list of some natural materials early settlers in the United States used for dyeing cloth. Here's a chance to try your own experimental archaeology.

In general the dye source must be heated to release its color, and a mordant must be added to set the dye so it will not fade. A mordant is usually a metallic compound that makes insoluble pools of dye in the fibers of the cloth. A list of mordants follows the list of dyes. You will need a large container to boil in and something (like a teeshirt — or a hard-boiled egg) to color.

Most of the old recipes go something like this. Put the dye source and mordant into your boiler, cover with water, and boil for a long time. Add your wet, unfolded cloth; and simmer until you get a color darker than that you want. Dry outside in a shady place.

If the recipe sounds vague, it is because most of your success with dyeing depends upon experimenting to get the results you want. So try it. And after you have tried these dye sources, you can try others and become more expert.

DYE SOURCES

1. Butternuts (green hulls) — black
2. Dandelion roots — light green
3. Field asters — gold
4. Goldenrod flowers (in bud) — orange
5. Grapes — rose to deep violet
6. Onion skins — yellow
7. Rock lichens — brownish orange
8. Tea or coffee — tan, brown
9. White birch (inner bark) — red

MORDANTS

1. Alum		5. Rusty nails
2. Baking soda		6. Salt
3. Chrome		7. Sulphur
4. Iron		8. Vinegar

The green hulls of these butternuts produce a black dye.

Do you see the hand in the picture? How many rings can you find? Do you recognize the vertebrae bones in the bottom right-hand corner?

10. Physical Anthropologist

Physical anthropology is the study of the physical characteristics of human beings. The physical anthropologist identifies human remains, mainly bones, and helps the archaeologist answer questions about early people.

What age and sex was the person? The skull development and shape and the kinds of teeth can give information about age. The pelvis, or hip bone, is an indicator of sex.

What did the person die from? Many accidents and even some diseases leave their mark on bone tissue.

116   If you check your library, you can track down answers to some of the questions that concern a physical anthropologist. What is the difference between the male and female pelvis? Where are ball and socket joints found in the human skeleton? Where are hinge joints and pivot joints found? How is an infant's skull different from an adult's?

In seventeenth century England a disease known as rickets was so common that it was considered normal. Rickets is a disease of the bones. If you knew how rickets affects the skeleton and what prevents the disease, you could tell a great deal about a group of skeletons whose bones were deformed by rickets.

Physical anthropologists are interested in the size and the structure of bones. These anthropologists want to know things like the capacity of the brain cavity.

When a skeleton is found, it is often important to determine the age at the time of death. With a tape measure and a few willing subjects, you can become fairly expert at judging a skeleton's age.

Start with yourself. You are surely much bigger than a one-year-old baby. But is every part of you much bigger? Get a tape measure and measure the length of a baby's head from chin to the top of the head. Measure from the top of the head to the bottom of the feet. Measure the head's circumference (distance around). Now perform the same measurements on yourself. Is your head much bigger than the baby's?

How big is your head in relation to the rest of your body? To find out, divide the size of your head into your total body length. You are trying to find out how many of your heads fit into your body length. Do the same division with the measurements you took of the baby. What do you notice?

You might like to extend your study. Try doing the same measurements on a newborn baby, a five-year-old, an adult, and a very old person. You are doing the kind of research that a physical anthropologist would do: collecting your own data and drawing conclusions from it.

11. Paleontologist

Paleontology deals with prehistoric life. Paleontologists study the fossil remains of plants and animals. Fossils are remains, such as skeletons, or impressions, such as footprints, in rock or in the ground that come from a former geological age. These fossils are perhaps the best evidence of the kinds of plant and animal life that existed during that period.

Paleontologists identify and catalog information about these very old forms of life. Paleontologists theorize about how the plants and animals lived, and how they came to be trapped and preserved by the rocky minerals.

Fossils are often found where water once covered the land. For example in the central United States you are likely to find fossilized remains of animals such as clams and fish. In some areas you might be lucky enough to find a few shark's teeth. As these animals died, they left their shells and skeletons on the bottom of the lake or ocean. Shells filled with silt and sand, and everything was covered layer by layer. In time this silt and sand turned to stone.

Try making your own fossils. You'll need plaster, modeling clay, a pencil, baby powder, and something to cast — like a scallop shell.

First form the clay into two slabs about three-quarters of an inch thick. Next sprinkle baby powder on the shell and on the clay slabs. The powder will keep the clay from sticking to the shell.

Press the scalloped, outer side of your shell into first one slab and then the other. You will have two hollowed-out, mirror images of your shell. Put one slab on top of the other, hollowed sides facing and matching like the two halves of a scallop. Carefully make a hole in the top of the clay with a pencil.

Mix the plaster according to the directions on the box, and pour this mixture into the hole until the mold is filled. Wait at

Paleontologists have found skeletons of Tyrannosaurus, a giant meat-eater who stood 18 feet high, 47 feet long and had a skull about four feet long.

least overnight before opening your cast to reveal the fossil inside. You can make molds of other solid animal remains, such as the bones of small animals.

Paleontologists are interested in the evolution of animal species. You may have heard of eohippus, the ancestor of the horse. Eohippus stood about 20 inches high, had toes instead of hoofs, and had teeth suitable for browsing on soft vegetation.

Many animals from the Pleistocene era were trapped in the tar pits of Rancho La Brea, California. These tar pits trapped many unwary animals, which may have mistaken the tar for water. Their struggles to free themselves drew other animals, like scavengers and predators, who in turn were trapped.

You may wish to do some reading about dinosaurs. In *National Geographic*, August 1978, an article entitled "A New Look at Dinosaurs" describes a relatively new theory that dinosaurs might well be the ancestors of today's birds. Read the evidence presented in the article and see if you agree.

12. Ceramist

The ceramist is an expert on ceramics, such as pottery, earthenware, tile, and porcelain. Since its beginnings, pottery has been one of the most common and yet most important artifacts that the archaeologist takes out of the ground. By comparing styles and variations of pottery, the archaeologist is able to date whole layers of soil and therefore the artifacts coming out of these layers.

The ceramist uses a number of clues for identifying pottery.

Shape and design   Shapes and designs were passed on with only slight changes through generations of potters. Then a new idea or technique would catch on, and a new style would become popular.

Potter's mark   Many potters and companies that made pottery placed an identification mark on their pottery.

Glaze   Different combinations of ground minerals can identify where and when a piece was made. Here is another opportunity for the archaeologist to practice experimental archaeology. Glazes can be mixed and fired using materials and techniques that would have been available to a particular group. Trying to duplicate the colors and textures of the artifacts taken from the ground can be quite a challenge.

Chemical content of the clay   Most soils are a mixture of chemicals, gravel, sand, silt, and clay in varied proportions. Early potters attempted to locate sites that had very high clay content because nonclay particles make clay hard to work.

Primitive people fired their clay to harden it and make it waterproof. Sometimes they placed their pots in a hole and built a fire on them. Sometimes pots were fired in stone kilns, or ovens.

One of the jobs of the ceramist is to piece together the broken sherds and glue them in place to reconstruct what the original object looked like. Often many of the pieces are missing, having been broken and lost. Putting broken pieces of pottery together is like doing a jigsaw puzzle in three, instead of two, dimensions.

Ask your parents for an old cup, saucer, or flowerpot that they won't mind your breaking. A chipped or cracked cup would be perfect. Place the object in a paper bag and strike it gently with a hammer or rock. (Your first project will be easier to put together if there are not more than fifty pieces.) After the object has been broken, gently shake the pieces in the bag; then throw away almost half of them to imitate the problem the ceramist faces. Now try to fit together the pieces left. Use little pieces of tape to hold the parts together until you have a good-sized piece that you can glue and put aside to dry.

Are there any identification marks on your object that might help you to determine where it was made? Figure out a way to estimate the original size of your object; as a guide, use only the pieces you have reconstructed.

Make Your Own Clay Pot

One of the earliest ways of shaping a pot or bowl was by building the object from clay coils. Try building a couple of vessels in different shapes. You might want to try a bowl, a cup, a pitcher, and a jug.

Begin by rolling out long snakes about a quarter inch to a half inch thick. You can make the bottom of your vessel by flattening a ball of clay and shaping it to the desired size. Coil a clay snake around the base and smooth the coil into the base with your finger. Place another coil on top of the first and smooth the second into the first inside and outside. You should not be able to see where the coils join unless you want to keep the outside joinings as decoration. Experiment with making the vessel narrower or wider by varying the size of the coils or by putting pressure on the clay to mold it into the desired shape. End your project by placing a rounded lip on the top edge to give it a finished look.

If your pot is made from a real clay which will eventually harden, you may want to try drying it outside in the warm air.

13. Epigrapher

Often archaeologists studying very ancient sites find clay tablets, statuary, or buildings with inscriptions carved into them. Epigraphers are experts in decoding ancient languages, a difficult job because many old languages are no longer spoken or written. The epigrapher must decode inscriptions symbol by symbol.

At times the archaeologist finds that no alphabet is involved. Instead the people may have used pictographs, picture symbols used to tell a story or honor an event. See if you can decode this pictographic story.

The words you use to tell the story may be different from the words someone else would use. Archaeologists have the same problem getting an exact meaning from pictographs. Only people who lived in the culture that produced the pictograph could know the exact meaning for sure because only they would share the understanding of what each symbol meant.

This illustration is from a thousand-year-old cave painting found in the Pecos River area of Texas.

The pictures tell of the shaman (priest or medicine man), who invokes the spirit of the hunt. The pictures show deer and possibly bear, which are being hunted with weapons such as arrows and arrow-thrower. Wheat and other foods used by these Indians are also pictured.

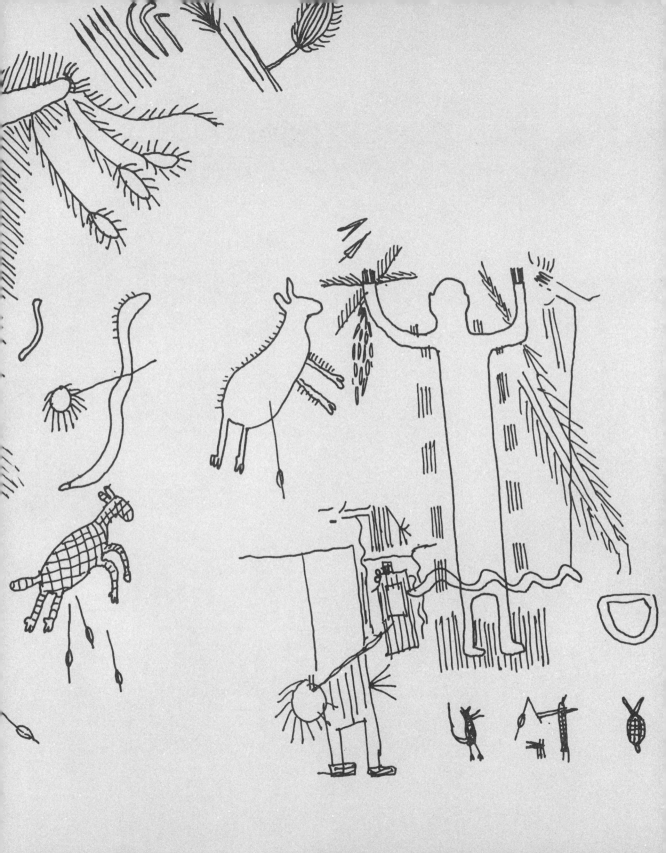

THE ROSETTA STONE

14. The Rosetta Stone

Sometimes the epigrapher is helped by the discovery of a key to the language. A key may come in the form of the same message's being written in more than one language. Such was the case in 1799 when an officer in the army of Napoleon discovered a large, black, basalt stone in the small town of Rosetta, Egypt. On the stone was a message carved in three languages.

The stone had been erected by the priests of Memphis to honor Ptolemy Epiphanes, King of Egypt, for his bounty to the temples and his attempts to improve the declining condition and prestige of Egypt. The message was written in hieroglyphics, the sacred characters of the priesthood; in demotic characters, the common or popular script of the day; and in Greek.

Scholars familiar with the Greek language were able to translate the decree with little trouble. By comparing the demotic text with Coptic — the modern language that came from ancient Egyptian — epigraphers were able to decipher the demotic text. The hieroglyphics were a bit more difficult until the experts realized that the signs were alphabetic and phonetic, not simply pictures representing ideas as was formerly thought.

The Rosetta Stone acted as the key to translating ancient Egyptian hieroglyphics.

15. A Challenge

Let's imagine that working with an inscription on an old gravestone, an epigrapher has been able to decipher a few letters of a newly discovered, ancient alphabet. The letters look like this:

B	O	R	N		D	I	E	D
T	I	Ш	A		Ɛ	V	J	Ɛ

An archaeologist, working at the site where this stone was discovered, has just sent the epigrapher two more objects with inscriptions. The objects, pictured in the illustration, seem to have their names inscribed across them.

If this is true, you should be able to use the clues provided to decode the following message. (Try it; then check your answers with the alphabet on the next page.)

16. Registrar

The registrar has a job much like that of a librarian. Like books and other materials in a library, all of the artifacts found during a dig must be carefully cataloged and stored. These records serve a twofold purpose. First the catalog makes it possible for the archaeologist to find a particular artifact. The catalog also serves to record artifacts sent for testing and identification. Second the catalog serves as a record of the artifacts and where they were found. Often studying these records helps the archaeologist to piece together relationships among artifacts, and therefore to understand the everyday lives of people who used them. Discovery of important activities performed by early peoples may depend upon the proper cataloging of materials from the field.

One of the skills that the registrar must practice is placing artifacts in categories that describe the material being cataloged. If you turn back to that wastebasket you worked with at the beginning of this book, you can try to place all of the objects into categories. Use categories such as paper, metal, food scraps, etc.

Make a list of all the materials under specific categories. Then try to divide each category into subcategories that describe the materials even more precisely. For instance, paper might be subdivided into paper with writing on it and paper without writing. You can then divide your subdivision of paper with writing on it into even finer subdivisions such as paper with writing that has a personal message, paper with writing that has a commercial message, and paper with writing that provides public information (for instance, a newspaper).

Subdivide each of your original categories as many times as possible and you will have some idea of what the registrar's job is like.

Each artifact, from the smallest to the largest, must be labeled with an identification number.

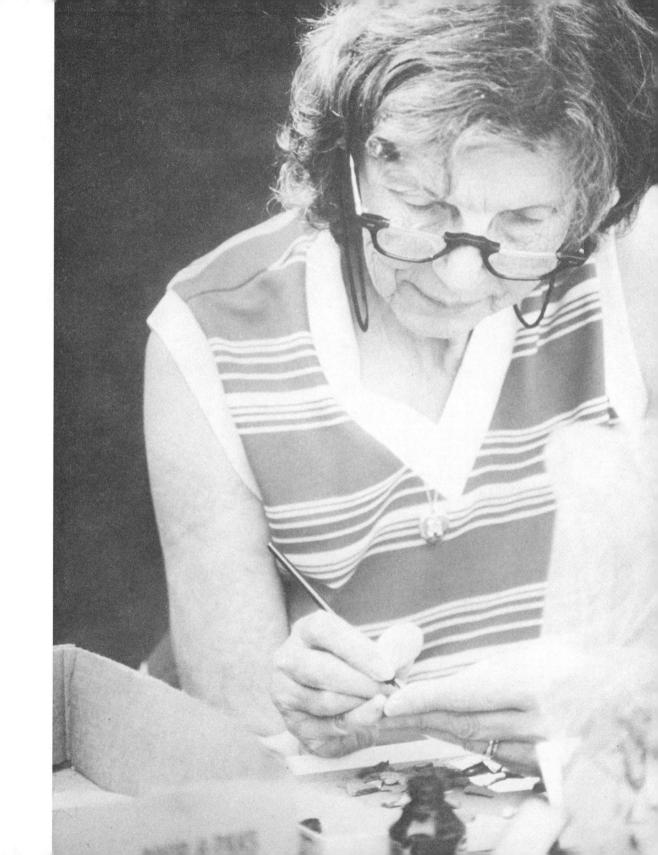

17. The Archaeologist's Report

All of the research, planning, digging, testing, and analysis of the artifacts leads to the most important part of the archaeologist's work — the written report. Without this last step, all of the information and work that have gone into the dig are lost to the world and will add nothing to our understanding of the past.

The archaeologist must take all of the raw data (artifacts, research, and reports from the various experts) and draw a picture of the people and their way of life. This activity is like solving a mystery story. Once the clues have been uncovered, we must figure out what took place.

18. The Mystery of the Boggy Bones

Several years ago while dragging a stream, a member of a gas drilling crew uncovered a few large bones of a kind he'd never seen. A call went in to a professor at the University of Wyoming. Here is what the professor found out after searching the area.

The bones belonged to a mammoth (mammathus columbi) and were about 11,000 years old. The body had been preserved in the black mud of a bog. Air and bacteria had been kept out by the bog so that everything was beautifully preserved. Also found in the mud were many stones the size of bowling balls, a large stone knife, a chopper, and a scraper.

Using just the information given to you here, what do you think might have happened 11,000 years ago at the site of this muddy bog?

It is not known whether the mammoth was driven into the bog or just wandered into it and was trapped. Once trapped, the mammoth was stoned by a small group of hunters. When there was no chance that the mammoth could free itself, the hunters stabbed it repeatedly and killed it. Then the hunters worked to save as much of the meat and hide as possible before the mammoth sank from sight. The June 1962 issue of *National Geographic* gives the full account.

19. The Mystery of the No-Cliff Hanger

After a particularly heavy rain an archaeologist surveying an area for evidence of early human activity came upon a piece of human skull and, not far from it, a stone spearhead partially uncovered by the rain. The archaeologist's preliminary map of the site showed that the artifacts were found fifteen feet from the base of a high cliff.

Back in the laboratory, the archaeologist was able to match the spearhead with a picture and description in a resource book. It identified the style and described the makers as an early hunting tribe that lived by following animals along their migratory routes. From this information the archaeologist decided that the area warranted further study.

A dig was begun. At the end of the dig, the archaeologist had gathered further information.

More human bones belonging to the original skull were found. All of them were found buried under a pile of stones, which the heavy rains had exposed. Many of the leg, hip, and chest bones were broken and crushed. The physical anthropologist identified the skeleton as that of a male, five feet three inches tall, probably weighing about one hundred thirty-five pounds.

Several more spearheads were found. Nearby were found other stone hand tools: thick-bladed knives and broader chisellike blades. The lithologist identified the chisel-bladed tools as hide scrapers.

Many large bones were uncovered. The zoologist identified them as belonging to a species of bison. The bones had been dismembered and scattered many feet from where they would have fallen had the animals died an undisturbed death. Many of the leg and skull bones had been crushed and broken.

134   A small fire hearth was located at the same level as the

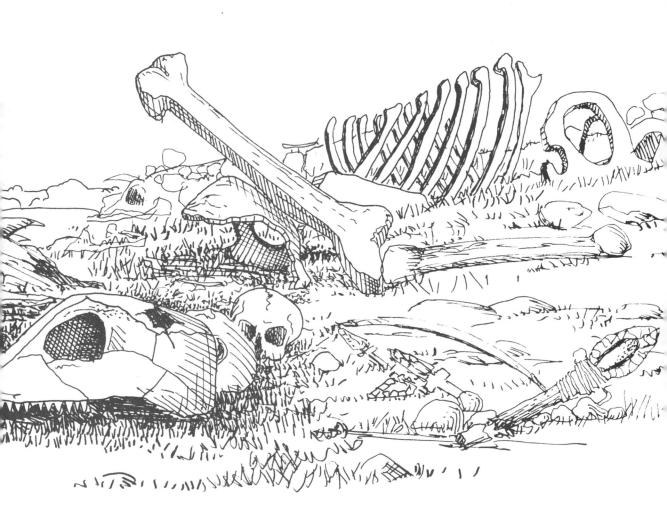

bones. Radio-carbon dating placed the charcoal at about 2,000
years old.

    Based on this information, what could have happened here?
When you have imagined this scene, look at the illustration on
the bottom of page 141 for one possible explanation.

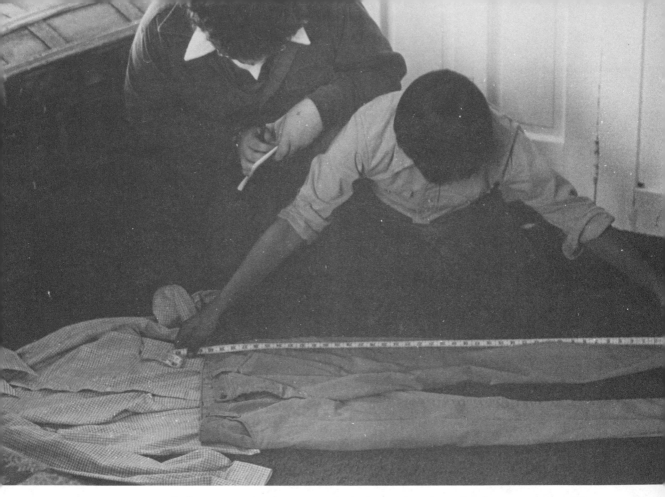

Jim and Shannon measure a set of clothing they have laid out to try to determine the owner's height and weight.

20. Reading Spaces

Reading Spaces is like reading a Sherlock Holmes story. The idea is to go somewhere that you've never been before and to discover everything you can about the place and the people who use it. This place could be an office, a home, a room at school, or a small store. Like Sherlock Holmes, you must look at everything as a potential clue to a mystery you are trying to solve.

Reading spaces is a lot of fun when done with a group. But

just as the archaeologist must get permission to survey a site, you must get permission to visit your site.

You will need a pad of paper, a pencil, and a tape measure. It will help you to get organized if you make a list of questions to be answered at your site. Imagine for the moment that you have chosen to visit a house belonging to people you have never met. What could you expect to find out about them?

People

How many? What are their ages? Names? What do they look like — height, weight, build, hair color? It is best if the people are not at home; but how then are you going to tell their heights, weights, builds, and hair colors? Try laying out a pair of pants and a shirt on a bed. Measure from the cuff of the pants to the collar of the shirt. Add a few inches for the feet. How large is the head going to be? (Use your research from the head-measuring activity to help you decide.) Using this method, you can probably come pretty close to guessing the person's correct height.

But the pants can tell you more. How big is the waistline? Compare that measurement with the person's height. Is the person thin, medium, or heavy for his or her height?

Now how are you going to figure out the color of the person's hair? Check the combs, brushes, and pillows. If you can't find a strand of hair, check photographs.

Try counting beds or toothbrushes to find out how many people live in the house.

What else could you try to find out about the people? Does any of them wear glasses? What kinds of jobs do the adults hold? Do the children attend school? If so, what grade are they in and what are they studying? What books, newspapers, and magazines do these people read? Do the magazines and books tell you anything about these people's interests? Are sports, crafts, or music among their hobbies or interests? Do these interests seem to be shared by the entire family?

All of these questions and more can be answered. How clever can you be at finding the clues?

Household

How are the pieces of furniture arranged in the rooms? The arrangement of furniture, ornaments, and magazines is as much an artifact as the articles themselves are. Which areas and articles in the house are decorative rather than useful? What types of food are eaten? What kind of cookware and dishes are used? Note the use of metals, plastics, wood, and other materials throughout the house. Are machines, such as a dishwasher or toaster, used to perform household activities? Is technology used for other purposes? How is the house heated? What type of fuel is used? How is energy obtained? How is water obtained? How are sewage, rubbish, and garbage disposed of? Are there any pets? What kinds? How many? What are their ages and sizes? A bowl on the kitchen floor or cat hairs on the couch are a dead giveaway.

House and Grounds. What kind of house is this? Identify its architectural type if possible. Were additions made to the house after it was built? Were any rooms in the house finished later than others? Are some rooms still unfinished? Is it possible to estimate the age of the house? How is space used in the house? Who uses which rooms the most? Has anything unusual, like flood or fire, happened to the house? Give a general description of the neighborhood. Is it rural or urban? A housing development or an apartment complex? What landscaping or gardening has been done? Are there recreation areas, such as swings, horseshoe stakes, or croquet hoops? Are there any out-buildings on the property? What is their design and what are they used for?

These are not the only discoveries that can be made if you're really looking. Good luck!

138   **Fitting the Pieces Together.** You've collected the data, the reports are in, and now you must figure out what it all means. Like the archaeologist, you have a lot of jigsaw puzzle pieces. When you fit them together, you will have a picture of the people and how they live. Like the archaeologist, you will find holes in your completed puzzle. Either you missed a clue or the clue wasn't there to find.

Your conclusions must be based upon the data that you collected. No fair guessing or taking things for granted just because you live in the time period that you are reading. Try to describe all members of the family. Include evidence for each statement you make about them. For instance, if you state that Bret, one of the children in the family, fishes for a hobby, your evidence includes finding fishing magazines in his bedroom, a fishing pole with his name printed on the handle, and a can of fresh worms near the pole.

The books people read often tell you something of their interests or hobbies.

Try to describe the daily life of this family. What does each of the family members do with his or her time? What activities do they enjoy together? What kind of neighborhood do they live in? Is it a complex culture or a very simple culture? What evidence do you have to support your conclusions?

Archaeologists' statements about a whole culture are not based on just one sample. You should try to show the same care in your statements.

Compare your conclusions with those of your friends. Does everybody interpret data in the same way? Do you think that all archaeologists interpret data in the same way? What kinds of things do you and your friends disagree on? You might find it fun to try to talk your friends into accepting your conclusions as correct. Let them argue their cases, too. Then try to get together and agree on as many points as possible. Do the group findings differ much from your personal findings?

Reading spaces offers you an opportunity to check your results. This is a privilege that the archaeologist does not normally enjoy. When your report and findings are complete, perhaps you can talk with one or more of the family members whose house you visited. This is the chance to check your results firsthand and rate yourself as an archaeological detective on your first dig.

AND NOW:

HAPPY DIGGINGS!

*One possible solution to the mystery of the No-Cliff Hanger
on pages 134 and 135.*

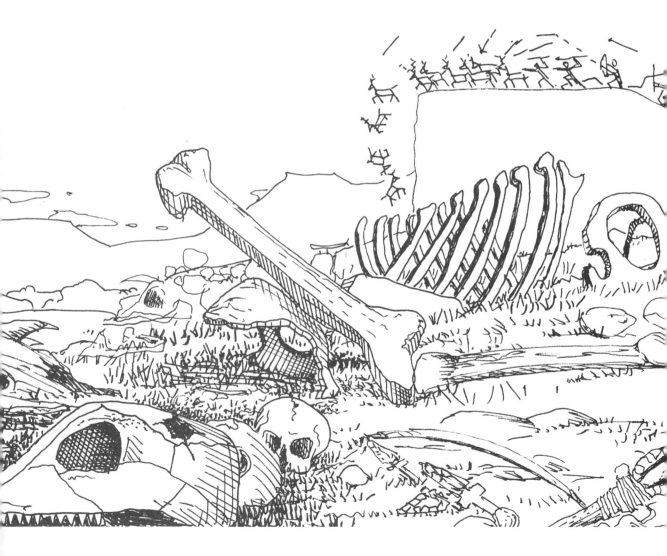

ADDRESSES

Addresses for specialty maps and test equipment

Topographical maps

Write for a catalogue of maps for your area.

U.S. Geological Survey
1200 South Eads Street
Arlington, Virginia 22202

Satellite photographs

Write for a catalogue ($1.25) for your area.

Geographic Computer Search
EROS Data Center
Sioux Falls, South Dakota 57198

A good place to get soil and water
testing equipment. Write for
their catalogue (50¢).

Edmund Scientific Company
EDSCORP Building
Barrington, New Jersey 08007

Addresses for State Archaeologists

Some states do not have a state archaeologist yet. If your state
does not appear in this list, which is alphabetical by state, write
to your governor to find out who is in charge of archaeological
work being done in your state.

Douglas Reger
State Archaeologist
Department of Natural Resources
323 East Fourth Avenue
Anchorage, Alaska 99501

Ronald Thomas
State Archaeologist
Hall of Records
Dover, Delaware 19901

Hester Davis
State Archaeologist
Arkansas Archaeological Survey
University of Arkansas
Fayetteville, Arkansas 72701

L. Rose Morrell
State Archaeologist
Florida Department of State
Tallahassee, Florida 32304

Frances Riddell
State Archaeologist
Department of Parks
   and Recreation
Box 2390
Sacramento, California 95811

Lewis Larson
State Archaeologist
Office of Planning and Research
Department of Natural Resources
270 Washington Street, SW
Atlanta, Georgia 30334

Bruce Rippeteau
State Archaeologist
Colorado State Museum
200 14th Avenue
Denver, Colorado 80203

Dr. James Kellar
State Archaeologist
Department of Anthropology
Indiana University
Bloomington, Indiana 47401

Douglas F. Jordan
State Archaeologist
University of Connecticut
Storrs, Connecticut 06268

Duane C. Anderson
State Archaeologist
University of Iowa
Iowa City, Iowa 52242

Thomas A. Witty
State Archaeologist
Kansas Historical Society
Tenth and Jackson Streets
Topeka, Kansas 66612

Dr. R. Berle Clay
State Archaeologist
University of Kentucky
Lexington, Kentucky 40506

Dr. William G. Haag
State Archaeologist
Louisiana State University
Baton Rouge, Louisiana 70803

Tyler Bastian
State Archaeologist
Maryland Geological Survey
Latrobe Hall,
    Johns Hopkins University
Baltimore, Maryland 21218

Maurice Robbins
State Archaeologist
Bronson Museum
8 North Main Street
Attleboro, Massachusetts 02703

John R. Halsey
State Archaeologist
Michigan History Division
208 North Capital Avenue
Lansing, Michigan 48918

Dr. Eldon Johnson
State Archaeologist
215 Ford Hall
University of Minnesota
Minneapolis, Minnesota 55455

Samuel McGahey
State Archaeologist
Department of Archives
    and History
Box 571
Jackson, Mississippi 39205

Stewart L. Peckham
State Archaeologist
Museum of New Mexico
Santa Fe, New Mexico 87501

Dr. Robert Funk
State Archaeologist
New York State Museum
Buffalo, New York 12222

Stephen J. Gluckman
State Archaeologist
Division of History and Archives
Archaeology Section
Raleigh, North Carolina 27611

Nick G. Franke
Research Archaeologist
State Historical Society
Bismarck, North Dakota 58501

Martha Potter Otto
Curator of Archaeology
Ohio Historical Center
Columbus, Ohio 43211

Don Wychoff
State Archaeologist
University of Oklahoma
Norman, Oklahoma 73069

Barry Kent
State Archaeologist
William Penn Memorial Museum
Box 1026
Harrisburg, Pennsylvania 17608

Robert L. Stephenson
State Archaeologist
Institute of Archaeology
  and Anthropology
University of South Carolina
Columbia, South Carolina 29208

Robert Alex
State Archaeologist
Archaeological Research Center
Box 152
Fort Meade, South Dakota 57741

Joseph L. Benthall
State Archaeologist
Department of Conservation
5103 Edmonson Pike
Nashville, Tennessee 37211

Curtis Tunnell
State Archaeologist
Box 12276, Capital Station
Austin, Texas 78711

David B. Madsen
State Archaeologist
603 East South Temple
Salt Lake City, Utah 84102

Giovanna Neudorfer
State Archaeologist
Division for Historic
  Preservation
Pavilion Building
Montpelier, Vermont 05602

Daniel Fowler
Archaeological Administrator
Geological and Economic
  Survey
Box 879
Morgantown, West Virginia 26505

Joan E. Freeman
State Archaeologist
Wisconsin Historical Society
816 State Street
Madison, Wisconsin 53706

George Frison
State Archaeologist
University of Wyoming
Laramie, Wyoming 82071

FURTHER READING

1. "A New Look At Dinosaurs" by John H. Ostrom, Ph.D., National Geographic Magazine, August 1978.

2. CLOCKS FOR THE AGES: HOW SCIENTISTS DATE THE PAST, Robert Silverburg, 1971, MacMillan Publishing Co. Inc., New York, N.Y.

3. THE LERNER ARCHAEOLOGY SERIES, DIGGING UP THE PAST, 1974, Lerner Publishing Co., Minneapolis, MN.

4. SCROUNGERS: THE STORY OF PREHISTORIC AMERICANS, R.H. Shimer, 1971, G.P. Putnam's and Sons, New York, NY.

5. THEY LIVED LIKE THIS IN THE OLD STONE AGE, Marie Neurath, 1971, Franklin Watts, Inc., New York, NY.

6. TREASURES OF YESTERDAY, Henry Garnett, Doubleday & Co., Garden City, NY.

7. THE WALLS OF WINDY TROY, a biography of Heinrich Schliemann by Marjorie Braymer, 1960, Harcourt Brace and Co., New York, NY.

8. "Wyoming Muck Tells of Battle; Ice Age Man Verses Mammoth" by Cynthia Irwin, Henry Irwin, and George Agogino, National Geographic Magazine, June 1962.

GLOSSARY

Archaeologist– a person who collects and studies the artifacts of our past and attempts to explain a people's way of life from this evidence.

Archaeology– the science of finding, collecting, and studying the material remains of our past.

Artifacts– the objects used by people in their everyday lives. This includes materials that people used even if they did not make the object (such as a large bone that was used for a club).

Balk– (balk wall) — a wall left between adjacent squares so that information taken from one will not be confused with information from the other.

Dowsing– searching for water or minerals by using a dowsing or devining rod.

Fossil– the hardened remains of some plant or animal from a different geological age.

Grid– a pattern of squares laid out over an area that is to be dug. Each square within the grid is numbered.

Locus– a place in a square that the archaeologist wants to make special note of. It might be a change in soil color or a special artifact. A new locus is given a number, measured carefully, and drawn in on the top plan. A soil sample is usually taken.

Necropolis– the cemetary of an ancient city. The "Valley of the Kings," where the rulers of ancient Egypt were buried, is a famous example.

Patish– a hand pick used for loosening the soil before it is scraped into a pile with the trowel.

Pollen – (pollen grain) — the yellow, fine-grained male sex cells found on the stamens of flowering plants.

Prehistoric – before the time of recorded history.

Sherd (pronounced shurd; alternate spelling *shard*) — a fragment of broken pottery.

Situ – Situ means place or position. "In Situ" is a phrase used by archaeologists to mean that an object is left in its original position, as information about it is gathered. In a photograph, an object might also be "in situ" or in place. Once it has been moved, an object is no longer in situ.

Square – a square area marked off with stakes and string in which the archaeologist digs.

Stratum – (plural, strata) — a horizontal layer of soil. Usually, the deeper the strata, the older the objects found in them.

Tell – in the Near East, these are places where cities were built upon the foundations of other cities until a great hill or mound was built up.

Top plan – a scale drawing of a square showing the positions of any important artifacts, large rocks, different soil colors, or anything that might be thought of importance to the clear reading of the square.

INDEX